IS THAT
YOUR FINAL
ANSWER?

IS THAT YOUR FINAL ANSWER?

Funny Answers to Quiz Show Questions

MYLES BYRNE

Michael O'Mara Books Limited

First published in Great Britain in 2020 by
Michael O'Mara Books Limited
9 Lion Yard
Tremadoc Road
London SW4 7NQ

A CIP catalogue record for this book is available from the British Library.

Papers used by Michael O'Mara Books Limited are natural, recyclable
products made from wood grown in sustainable forests. The manufacturing
processes conform to the environmental regulations of the country of
origin.

ISBN: 978-1-78929-272-5 in paperback print format
ISBN: 978-1-78929-274-9 in ebook format

1 2 3 4 5 6 7 8 9 10

Illustrations by Andrew Pinder
Designed and typeset by D23
Printed and bound by CPI Group (UK) Ltd, Croydon, CR0 4YY

www.mombooks.com

CONTENTS

Introduction: Blankety Blank Minds	7
What Were They Thinking About?	11
Double Acts I	20
Double Acts II	27
The Natural World and Some Asparagus	32
There's Something About Paris	39
And Not Just Paris . . . Beyond	44
The Trouble with Celebrities and TV	52
Celebrity Fails	58
Quickfire Round I	66
And Now to Monty . . .	70
Fun with Formats	78
Golden Gogan	86
The *Blockbusters* Chronicles and Golden Oldies	94
Quickfire Round II	103
Name Something That . . .	107
So Wrong They're Almost Right	116
So Close, Yet So Far . . .	124
Who isn't Going to be a Millionaire? I	131
Millionaire II – Fastest Fingers and Clangers	141
Quickfire Round III	151

What Would Will Have Said?   155

And as for Music . . .   163

Early Morning Blues   169

More Innuendo: *Family Feud* and *Countdown*   179

The Three 'R's – Reading, Riting and Rithmetic   186

Quickfire Round IV   194

Wheel of Moron   199

A Brief History of the World   206

Everybody Needs Good Neighbours   214

Calling Captain Obvious   220

Desperate Measures   227

Man, the Rational Animal   236

Maths, *Millionaire* and Good Humour   243

Universally Challenged   249

Family Feud Revisited   254

A Final Thought   267

Acknowledgements   269

INTRODUCTION:
BLANKETY BLANK MINDS

We've all been there. It might have been when you gave a speech in front of a crowd, were in front of an intimidating interview panel or it was a horribly awkward first date.

Even if you start out feeling confident, it just takes that one moment of doubt and suddenly your mind is in a whirl: your palms start sweating, your knees start to shake, eyes swivel . . . And then you actually hear what you're saying. Drivel!

Someone has asked you a question. You have to say *something* . . . And you blurt out the first thing that comes into your mind, which turns out to be completely idiotic and bonkers. Or the correct answer may genuinely be on the tip of your tongue but, at the last minute, you convince yourself it was a trick question and what comes out of your mouth is totally, outrageously . . . *weird*.

So, imagine how much more intense that sense of panic must be if you are on a TV quiz show under bright, hot lights, with producers frantically gesturing in the corner of your eye – 'OMG, cut to a commercial, quick, now, NOW' – and a studio audience is giggling at your blatant, embarrassing discomfort. Because you know that everyone you've ever met, ever wanted to impress, is watching totally gobsmacked. Or listening live on the radio.

Of course, before the internet you might have got away with it. If your boss or the Hot One you're aching to ask out on a date hadn't seen it, yes, they might later hear what happened but you can always laugh it off. Turn yourself into the hero. And anyway, they'd forget. Remember the man whose performance on the 1980s game show *Family Fortunes* (ITV) became legendary when, having heard the word 'chicken' shortly before he took to the stage, inexplicably answered every question with 'turkey'. Well, his family and friends would have remembered his embarrassment alright, but the wider world, no way. And then arrived . . . the internet.

These days, your minor pieces of idiocy can end up being enshrined for everyone's entertainment, in Russia, China, you name it. You go viral on social media. Your twitching, squirming, floundering performance is enshrined for the rest of your life, a comic must-see with shame and stupidity that gets retweeted even by Donald Trump. Which reminds me of the contestant who, on being asked to name people whose last name was 'Obama', blurted out 'bin Laden'. Or the ex-England cricketer, Monty Panesar, who tried to avoid letting his family and friends watch his hapless BBC *Mastermind* performance by taking them out to dinner on the night of the broadcast. Except they heard soon enough and watched again and again *and again* the entire travesty on YouTube the following day.

The German word *schadenfreude* means 'taking pleasure in someone else's misfortune'. And one of the pleasures of watching a quiz show is sitting smugly at home, safely out of the TV lights, with a cup of tea and enjoying a deep, abiding sense of *schadenfreude* as the contestants struggle to answer the simplest of questions. Then you can casually say to yourself 'I knew that', even if you really, really didn't.

In addition to the questions to which contestants have unwittingly given utterly bizarre answers, we also explore the sections on game shows that are intentionally designed to elicit embarrassing and/ or comical answers. This ranges from *Family Feud* (CBS) in the US, to shows like *Blankety Blank* (BBC; aka *The Match Game* on NBC, CBS and ABC) in which celebrity participants are explicitly there to provide entertaining ripostes: we've included some of the classic moments from these shows on the basis that, while not technically stupid, they are most definitely funny.

Our researchers have watched thousands of hours of game shows to find some of the most idiotic moments, and now we have compiled them for your entertainment . . . Enjoy!

WHAT WERE THEY THINKING ABOUT?

Sigmund Freud introduced us to the idea that the things we say, especially slips of the tongue, can be highly revealing about what is actually going on in the subconscious. And these Freudian slips on game shows can sometimes leave you wondering what on earth is actually going on in the contestant's mind. So, let's begin with:

From *University Challenge* (BBC)

Jeremy Paxman: Thuma, Towcher, Long-man, Lech-man and Little-man are Old and Middle English names for which parts of the human body?*
King's College School of Medicine Contestant: Penis?

Paxman: You're a medical student – how many penises did they teach you we have nowadays?!

* The correct answer was 'Fingers'.

Paxman: What is another name for 'cherrypickers' and 'cheesemongers'?
Contestant: . . . Homosexuals?

Paxman: No. They're regiments in the British Army, who will be *very* upset with you.

From *Family Feud* (CBS)

Steve Harvey: Name something a burglar wouldn't want to see when he breaks into a house.
Contestant: Naked grandma!

Harvey: . . . Naked, huh . . .
Contestant: I don't want to see that, neither.

Harvey: I know you're right, OK? Uh . . . Nobody wants to see a naked grandma, but . . . what are the chances . . . of you breaking into a house and runnin' into your grandmama naked, at home?*

* Harvey's merriment was cut short when it was revealed that this was technically a correct answer since a 'grandma' could count as an 'occupant'.

Richard Dawson: Name a department in a supermarket.
Contestant: Lingerie.

From *The Weakest Link* (BBC)

Anne Robinson: What is the full name of Karl Marx's book, *Das . . . ?*

Contestant: *Kampf.**

* It's interesting to see the thought process, which managed to jump from Marxism to National Socialism and then to a correct answer . . . to the wrong question. And worth noting that a similar problem presumably afflicted a contestant who, when asked to name the allied leader who met with Roosevelt and Stalin at Yalta in 1945, came up with 'Hitler'!

Robinson: What 'T' are people who live in a house paying rent to a landlord?

Contestant: Terrorists.

Robinson: What 'A' is a small, dead-end tube in the digestive system with no known function?

Contestant: Arse.

You have to worry about this contestant who clearly liked conspiracy theories and the idea that space exploration was the special domain of the Nazis:

Robinson: Space exploration. What does the acronym NASA stand for?

Contestant: National Socialist Space Satellite.

From *Jeopardy!* (CBS)

Bear in mind that, on this show, you sometimes need to provide the question to match the answer you are given . . .

> **Host:** The answer is, 'This term for a long-handled gardening tool can also mean an immoral pleasure seeker.'*
> **Contestant:** What is a hoe?

* The correct answer is 'What is a rake?'

From *Wheel of Fortune* (CBS)

Contestants need to guess the correct letters to complete a familiar phrase: on one show, the contestants had reached a point where only one more letter was required.

A STREETCAR NA_ED DESIRE

> **Contestant:** [hesitantly, looking embarrassed] . . . 'K'?

In this game, the initial board read:

T _ E
_ _ R _ _ _ L _ S

Which isn't easy to guess. However, after a few letters had been chosen, things were clearer:

T _ E

_ C R O P O L _ S

At this point, the next contestant had ten seconds to guess the phrase, which really should have taken one second:

Contestant: Errr [worrying pause] . . . Tie Acropolis? Toe Acropolis . . . Tee Acropolis . . . [buzzer sounds for 'Time's up']

Another lovely moment from *Wheel of Fortune* came when the correct answer was 'A group of well-wishers'. After one contestant had won some money by correctly guessing a 'P' would be in the answer, the board read:

_ _ R _ _ P _ _

_ _ _ _ - _ _ S H _ R S

Not much to go on, but the contestant's inspired guess of 'A group of pill-pushers' led to widespread hilarity and, given that it is a family show broadcast before the watershed, a gentle reminder from host Pat Sajak that 'This is *Wheel of Fortune!*'

From *Family Fortunes* (ITV)

Host: Name one of the seven wonders of the world.

Contestant: Dopey?

From *Family Feud* (CBS)

Host: Name a part of the body that might get pulled.

Contestant: Penis . . . ?

Host: [looking gobsmacked]

Contestant: . . . Nipples?

Host: [pauses for two seconds trying not to laugh, then walks off the set, unable to retain his composure]

Speaking of which, there is a lovely moment from the UK game show *Pointless* (BBC) in which the contestant is attempting to name the Commissioner of the Metropolitan Police, Cressida Dick, but unfortunately remembers her name as 'Caressa Dick'. In spite of repeated, urbane prompts from host Alexander Armstrong ('Hmmm . . . Caressa Dick . . . are you sure you want to go with that?') he insists on sticking with his answer.

From *Blankety Blank* (BBC)

Host: First thing in the morning I usually find my husband's blank on her blank.
Contestant (an elderly gentleman): I'd probably find my teeth on her sink.

From *Match Game* (CBS)

This 1970s US game show, hosted by Gene Rayburn, became *Blankety Blank* in Australia and then the UK.

Gene Rayburn: What is the longest bone in the human body?

Male Contestant: Tibia [he was close because the femur is the longest and the tibia is the second longest].

Rayburn: [turns to female contestant and repeats the question]
Female Contestant: [looks desperate] . . . Labia?

Host: Name an activity that is both healthy and fun.
Contestant: Sex.

Host: Name something that rhymes with 'coke'.
Contestant: 'Toke'?

From BBC Radio York

Jonathan Cowap: If someone is described as 'hirsute', what are they?
Contestant: Erm . . .

Cowap: Here's a clue – most men are, and most women would like us to think they are not.
Contestant: Is it gay, Jonathan?

Cowap: No.

It's also worth bearing in mind that our ignorance of religion is pretty all-encompassing, as witnessed by this very forgiving moment:

From *The Lunchtime Show* (BRMB Radio)

Host: What religion was Guy Fawkes?
Contestant: Jewish.

Host: That's close enough!

From *The Janice Forsyth Show*
(BBC Radio Scotland)

Janice Forsyth: What is the currency in India?
Contestant: Ramadan?

Even that staggering moment was trumped by the caller to the BBC2 show *See Hear on Saturday*, who was asked what country the spiritual leader the Dalai Lama comes from and, after a momentary pause, answered – 'Scotland'.

DOUBLE ACTS I

The US edition of *Celebrity Squares*, *Hollywood Squares* (NBC) used to be enhanced by the brilliant comic timing and imagination of Paul Lynde, a camp actor best known for playing Uncle Arthur in *Bewitched* (ABC), as well as being the snarky voice of numerous cartoon characters. At one point the issue was the slightly dubious question, 'Are women still attractive to men after they have had children?' Putting aside the political incorrectness, Lynde's answer, which reduced the panel and host to tears of laughter, was to pause and innocently say, 'What? Do you mean right after?'

A large part of *Hollywood Squares* consisted of feeder lines that were designed to invite humorous responses from the panel of celebrities, but Lynde's contributions to the show always stood out from the crowd as comedy gold. Here are a few of his greatest hits with the host, Peter Marshall:

Peter Marshall: If the right part comes along, will George C. Scott do a nude scene?
Paul Lynde: You mean he doesn't have the right part?

Marshall: Will a goose help warn you if there's an intruder on your property?
Lynde: There's no better way!

Marshall: What is a pullet?
Lynde: A little show of affection . . .

Marshall: In the Middle Ages, Paul, people in convents were not allowed to eat beans because they believed something about them we now know isn't true. What?
Lynde: Well, I know they took a vow of silence . . .

Marshall: In *Alice in Wonderland*, who kept crying 'I'm late, I'm late?'
Lynde: Alice, and her mother is sick about it.

Marshall: Prometheus was tied to the top of a mountain by the gods because he had given something to man. What did he give us?
Lynde: I don't know what you got, but I got a sports shirt.

Marshall: When Richard Nixon was vice-president, he went someplace on a 'goodwill mission', but instead wound up being stoned and shouted at. Where did this take place?
Lynde: Pat's room [Pat was Nixon's wife].

Marshall: True or false, cow's horns are used to make ice cream.

Lynde: You mean those weren't chocolate chips?

Marshall: Paul, why do Hell's Angels wear leather?

Lynde: Because chiffon wrinkles too easily.

Marshall: What are 'dual-purpose' cattle good for that other cattle aren't?

Lynde: They give milk and cookies . . . but I don't recommend the cookies.

Marshall: Diamonds should not be kept with your family jewels, why?

Lynde: They're so cold!

Marshall: According to the American cookery writer, Julia Child, how much is a pinch?
Lynde: Just enough to turn her on . . .

Marshall: True or false? Research indicates that Columbus liked to wear bloomers and long stockings.
Lynde: It's not easy to sign a crew up for six months . . .

Marshall: It is considered in bad taste to discuss two subjects at nudist camps. One is politics. What is the other?
Lynde: Tape measures.

Marshall: It used to be called '9-pin'. What's it called today?
Lynde: Foreplay!

Marshall: True or false? The navy has trained whales to recover objects a mile deep.
Lynde: At first they tried unsuccessfully with Cocker Spaniels.

Marshall: When you pat a dog on its head he will usually wag his tail. What will a goose do?
Lynde: Make him bark.

Marshall: Paul, in the early days of Hollywood, who was usually found atop Tony, the Wonder Horse?
Lynde: My Friend Flicka.

Marshall: Burt Reynolds is quoted as saying, 'Dinah [Shore] is in top form. I've never known anyone to be so completely able to throw herself into a . . .' A what?

Lynde: A headboard.

Marshall: In one state, you can deduct $5 from a traffic ticket if you show the officer . . . what?

Lynde: A $10 bill.

Marshall: What is the name of the instrument with the light on the end that the doctor sticks in your ear?

Lynde: Oh, a cigarette.

Marshall: True or false? Each generation of Americans has been about an inch taller than the previous generation.
Lynde: That makes [fellow panellist] Robert Conrad an antique!

Marshall: It's well known that small amounts of female hormones are found in the male body. Are male hormones ever found in the female body?
Lynde: Occasionally . . .

Marshall: In *The Wizard of Oz*, the lion wanted courage and the tin man wanted a heart. What did the scarecrow want?
Lynde: He wanted the tin man to notice him.

Marshall: Snow White . . . was she a blonde or a brunette?
Lynde: Only Walt Disney knows for sure.

Marshall: Billy Graham recently called it 'our great hope in a confusing and ever-changing world'. What is it?
Lynde: Pampers.

Marshall: How many men are on a hockey team?
Lynde: Oh, about half.

Marshall: What should you do if you're going 55 miles per hour and your tyres suddenly blow out?
Lynde: Honk if you believe in Jesus!

Marshall: We've all heard the old phrase 'A pig in a poke'. What is a poke?

Lynde: It's when you're not really in love.

Marshall: Is it normal for Norwegians to talk to trees?

Lynde: As long as that's as far as it goes.

Marshall: Paul, in what famous book will you read about a talking ass who wonders why it's being beaten?

Lynde: I read it, *The Joy of Sex*.

Marshall: Paul, this is for $1,200 and the championship. Dale Evans recently revealed the three secrets behind her happy marriage with Roy Rogers. Now listen carefully . . . 'We work together, we pray together and we're darn good . . .' What?

Lynde: In the saddle.

DOUBLE ACTS II

One of the greatest extended quiz show fails ever on the radio was on *Hold Your Plums* (Radio Merseyside), presented by Billy Butler and Wally Scott for ten years. The silly, anarchic quizzes were often enlivened by the hosts' obvious giggling at the absurdity of their contestants' confusion.

It can add to the hilarity of a quiz show when the host bends over backwards to give the contestants a hint, but all efforts fall on deaf ears. The same is true when the answer is achingly obvious – even being highlighted in the question – but the contestant is still left flummoxed and floundering.

On one occasion they asked a local caller what Walter Raleigh had brought back from the New World apart from tobacco (the correct answer was 'potatoes'). Her first guess was 'bowls', at which they had some fun discussing the difference between Sir Walter Raleigh and Sir Francis Drake.

Then they gave her another chance, with the muttered aside 'If she says "a bicycle", I'll kill her . . .' (Raleigh is a well-known British bike brand). She didn't make that mistake but was still stumped, so they resorted to giving her clues to each syllable in turn.

First they asked about her husband's stomach, in an attempt to tease out the idea of a 'pot-belly'. After going down a long rabbit hole involving pans and all kinds of cooking equipment, they eventually changed tack and succeeded in getting her to guess the word 'top' and then reverse it to . . . 'pot'.

For the second syllable they asked her for the number after seven, but they had a false start on the last syllable after asking, 'What's at the end of your feet?' to which she answered, 'Me slippers.' But finally, *finally*, five minutes into the call, they got her to guess the third syllable, 'toes'.

Clearly relieved, they asked her to say all the syllables in a row:

Caller: Pot. Eight. Toes.

Billy Butler: Yes! Yes!

Caller: Yes?

Butler: So, what were they [that Walter Raleigh] brought back?

Caller: I don't know!

Butler: You've just told me! . . . Good God, woman, you've just told me!

Caller: Pot. Eight. Toes . . . Potty-toes?

Butler: Yes!

Caller: Well, I don't know what they are! [extended laughter all round, including the caller]

Wally Scott: Give her a clue, Bill.

Butler: How can I give her a clue?! She's got it!
Caller: But I don't know . . .

Butler: 'I want you to tell me what they are! POT
. . . EIGHT . . . TOES . . . Say it very slow.
Caller: Pot . . . Eight . . . Toes.

Butler: Yes. Now what are they?
Caller: I don't know . . . you keep saying and I
don't know . . . I've never heard of the word.

And Talking of Spuds . . .

Clearly, plenty of people have problems with potatoes. One *Family Feud* (CBS) contestant had to name a famous word or phrase that started with the word 'Pot', to which the top answers were actually 'Pot luck', 'Pothead' and 'Pot pie'. In spite of heavy hints from the host Steve Harvey ('Yes, ma'am . . . we all know it starts with "Pot", but we all KNOW no one says "Pot-a-to". . .') she insisted on sticking with her doomed choice and ended up with zero points.

And here's another from *Family Feud*:

Steve Harvey: Name a reason the coroner might suspect someone's not dead, but just sleeping.
Contestant: I'm gonna have to go . . . with potato [he is congratulated by the family member next to him, who says 'Good answer'].

Harvey: There are millions of people at home watching this right now. The two of you are the only ones who think that's on that damn board. Potato!

And finally . . .

Host: Name a drink you recognize by its smell.
Contestant: Potatoes.

From *The Phil Wood Show* (BBC Radio)

Phil Wood: What 'K' could be described as the Islamic Bible?
Contestant: Er . . .

Wood: It's got two syllables . . . Kor . . .
Contestant: . . . Blimey?

Wood: [laughs awkwardly] The past participle of run . . .
Contestant: . . .

Wood: OK, let's try that another way. Today I run, yesterday I . . .
Contestant: Ah . . . walked?

THE NATURAL WORLD AND SOME ASPARAGUS

These days we often live in lifeless, urban environments, with little or no nature surrounding us. It is nonetheless dispiriting to see how little many quiz contestants know about the natural world, and that quiz contestants think, for instance, that an insect commonly found hovering over a lake is called a 'crocodile', that the animal that builds dams and lodges is a 'sheep', or that cumulus and cirrus are types of 'lion'. And the natural ignorance doesn't end there. Read on:

From *The Weakest Link* (BBC)

Anne Robinson: What is the correct name for the Australian wild dog?
Contestant: The dingbat.

Robinson: What does a bat use to facilitate flying in the dark?
Contestant: Its wings.

Robinson: Which bird gives its name to a straight-legged marching step?
Contestant: The cuckoo.

Robinson: In the animal kingdom, what 'C' is a large North American reindeer?
Answer: A moose.

Robinson: The name of which small, wingless, jumping insect precedes 'bite', 'collar' and 'market' to give three familiar terms?
Contestant: Bicycle.

From *Friends Like These* (BBC)

Ian Wright: What type of creature is a praying mantis?
Contestant: . . . A fish.

Wright: [trying to keep a poker face] Are you *sure* you want to say fish?
Contestant: [without hesitation] Yes, a fish.

Host: Name something a rabbit might do in a magician's hat.
Contestant: Fly away!

Steve Harvey: Name something that follows the word 'pork'.
Contestant: Cupine.

From *Wheel of Fortune* (CBS)

Presented with the following letters from a famous phrase, one contestant came up with one of the more surreal guesses of all time:

- O - E Y S - C K - E B - S - *

Contestant: Popsicle Bike!

* The correct answer was Honeysuckle bush.

From *The Chase* (ITV)

Bradley Walsh: A Peking bird, which is used in a famous Chinese dish?
Contestant: Parrot.

Walsh: Parrot? Peking Parrot? It's DUCK!

From *Pointless* (BBC)

Alexander Armstrong: What bird is most associated with the sound twit-twoo?

Contestant: Cockatoo.

And now for some snappy Q's and As:

Q: What is the name of the insect which makes honey?

A: Honey Fly.

Q: Macaws are from which family of birds?

A: Kestrels.

Q: The principal characters in the book *Watership Down* are what type of creatures?

A: Beavers.

Q: According to the popular wartime song, which birds will be over the white cliffs of Dover?
A: Jailbirds.

Q: What insect has many limbs, although the name would suggest that it has one hundred?
A: A giraffe.

Q: The llama and alpaca are related to which humped animal of South Asia and North Africa?
A: Hippo.

Q: What creature has a variable number of legs whose name derives from 'a thousand feet'?
A: Octopus.

Q: Which animals build dams and lodges?
A: Sheep.

* * *

PINK FLAMINGOS

The US game show *1 vs 100* (NBC) starts with 100 contestants and whittles them down to a winner, with progressively more difficult multiple-choice questions. On one show the first question was 'Why is a flamingo pink?' The three possible answers were:

1. Their diet
2. Embarrassment
3. Forgot to put on sunblock

And 32 out of 100 contestants were eliminated after they somehow managed to choose the wrong one!

* * *

And now, believe it or not, some asparagus, a vegetable that most people either love or hate; it occupies a strange corner of the human psyche. When confronted with a question that discombobulated them, a surprising number of people gave asparagus as the answer. Why, oh why, OH WHY?

Host: Name a food that comes in instant form.
Contestant: Asparagus.

Host: Name something you wouldn't want to find in the boot of your car.
Contestant: Asparagus.

However, sometimes asparagus gets the last laugh, as shown in this exchange from *Family Fortunes* (BBC):

Host: Name something that gets dried up when it's old.
Contestant: Asparagus.

Host: [he gave this answer the full works of derisive looks and eye-rolling before the answer board vindicated the contestant by revealing 'fruit and vegetables' as the top answer with 44 per cent]

THERE'S SOMETHING ABOUT PARIS

In the movie *Sabrina,* Audrey Hepburn's character has the well-known line, 'Paris is always a good idea . . .' Well, for some reason, when quiz show contestants are asked pretty much any question about European countries, the only good idea they seem to have is to randomly blurt out 'Paris!' or, occasionally, 'France!' Here are a few of the more egregious Parisian moments:

From *Are You Smarter than a 5th Grader?* (Fox)

Host: Which European country is Budapest the capital of?

Contestant: This might be a stupid question. I thought Europe was a country? I know they speak French there, don't they? Is France a country?

From *Family Fortunes* (ITV)

Les Dennis: Name a foreign country where it would be easy to put on weight.
Contestant: Paris.

From *The Weakest Link* (BBC)

Anne Robinson: In which continent is the River Danube?
Contestant: France.

From *Pointless* (BBC)

Bear in mind that contestants on this show compete in pairs, which seems like an excellent way to ruin a beautiful friendship.

Contestant one: [explains she has lots of different interests and 'stuff']

Alexander Armstrong: Now, does any of that include a knowledge of countries that end in two consonants?
Contestant one: No.

Armstrong: [sadly] Ohhh.
Contestant one: I did Geography at A level, but that's about as far as it goes [nervous laugh].

Armstrong: Yes . . .
Contestant one: [spreading her arms in confusion] Paris?

Contestant two: [looks at Contestant one in shock then looks away and rolls her eyes]

Contestant one: Oh . . . I don't know, I can't think . . . of anything. I've gone blank . . .

Armstrong: [unctuously] Don't worry, don't worry at all . . . I really don't mind . . .

Contestant two: [says nothing, but rolls her eyes again and assumes a 1000-yard stare into the distance]

From *Family Feud* (CBS)

Host: Name a country you'd like to visit if you spent a summer in Europe.
Contestant: Paris.

From *The Late Show* (BBC Midlands Radio)

Alex Trelinski: What is the capital of Italy?
Contestant: . . . France.

Trelinski: France is another country. Try again.
Contestant: . . . Oh, um . . . Benidorm.

Trelinski: Wrong, sorry. Let's try another question. In which country is the Parthenon?
Contestant: Sorry . . . I don't know.

Trelinski: Just guess a country, then.
Contestant: . . . Paris!

From *Wheel of Fortune* (CBS)

Assistant reveals prize that a husband and wife have won a gondola ride through Venice.

Host: Let's check your geography . . . What country do you think we are sending you to?

Husband: Paris? [prompting collective laughter, especially from wife]

Husband: France!

Wife: [still laughing] Do we still get it? [and yes, they still got the prize]

From *In It to Win It* (BBC)

Note that the only answer the following question actually needs is 'Yes'.

> **Dale Winton:** Alderney and Sark – are they part of the Channel Islands?
> **Contestant:** Oooh! Is that the English Channel? I don't know, are there islands in the English Channel? I've never heard of any. France . . . that's near the English Channel, isn't it?

And finally, if you are ever on a TV quiz show, do bear in mind that sometimes the answer really is Paris:

From *The Richard and Judy Show* (ITV)

> **John Leslie:** What is the capital of France?
> **Contestant:** [excruciating pause] . . . Belgium.

AND NOT JUST PARIS...
BEYOND

That Paris problem is a good example of quiz contestants' shocking lack of knowledge of world geography. We've always known that many Americans have no passport and no interest in the world beyond their borders, but it is not just Americans who know zilch about the Great Beyond.

For the first few questions, which come from BBC's *The Weakest Link*, bear in mind that Anne Robinson was one of the harshest hosts in quiz show history. Rather than expressing sympathy for, or finding humour in, the contestants' mistakes, she relentlessly mocked them, taking on a pseudo-dominatrix persona, upholding the show's schtick of eliminating the most useless contestant, round by round. Her scornful face was something to behold when, for instance, a contestant told her that Australia is the country whose capital is 'Wellington', or that the city in which you would find the Kremlin building is 'Russia'. And that's not to mention the contestants who thought that the capital of Iraq was 'Iran', that 'Canada' was the last state to join the United States of America or that a South American country that has borders with ten other countries might just be 'China'.

You can't even count on contestants knowing the difference between a salad dip and a country, as demonstrated on *The Vault* (ITV) when Melanie Sykes asked, 'What's a mixture of avocado, chili and lime juice commonly known as?' and the contestant confidently stated, 'Guatemala'! And now:

From *The Weakest Link* (BBC)

Robinson: So, Gemma, for £9,350, which is the largest and most heavily populated island in the Mediterranean Sea?
Contestant: Spain.

Robinson: Which oriental country shares its name with a type of porcelain?
Contestant: Portugal.

Robinson: What 'K' is the currency of Sweden?
Contestant: . . . Kennel?

Robinson: Pakistan was part of which other state before it achieved independence in 1947?
Contestant: Bulgaria.

Robinson: Which city was chosen as the host city for the first Chinese Grand Prix in 2007?
Contestant: Tokyo.

Robinson: Which German city is also the name of a type of perfume?
Contestant: . . . Berlin?

Robinson: In Asian geography, Vietnam has borders with Cambodia, Laos and which other country?
Contestant: America.

Robinson: A Catalan is an inhabitant of a region in Spain known in English as what?
Contestant: Catatonia.

Robinson: Sri Lanka is situated to the south-east of which Asian country?
Contestant: South Africa.

Robinson: Gotham is not only a place in the Batman series, but also a city in which European country?
Contestant: Italy.

Robinson: In what language, spoken in part of the United Kingdom, was the hymn *Guide Me O Thou Great Redeemer* originally written?
Contestant: Islam.

Robinson: What is the capital of Saudi Arabia?
Contestant: . . . Tel Aviv?

From *Are You Smarter Than a 5th Grader* (Fox)

Host: Name a country where everyone speaks French.
Contestant: Europe.

From *Tipping Point* (ITV)

Ben Shephard: Between 1991 and 1999, Peter Schmeichel was the goalkeeper for which English football club?
Contestant: Germany?

Would it make me sound like part of the metropolitan elite if I suggested that local radio also provides particularly fertile ground for geographical ignorance? If so, don't worry, I'm writing this in a pair of last week's pants and smoking a fag while *This Morning* is playing in the background. So, let's start with:

From *Notts and Crosses* (BBC Radio Nottingham)

Jeff Owen: In which country is Mount Everest?

Contestant: [extended silence] Ummm . . . it's not in Scotland, is it?

Host: In which country would you find Miami?

Caller: Ermmm . . . pass.

Host: So, this is a first-grade question . . . Name a continent.

Contestant: The United States?

From Lincs FM phone-in

Host: Which is the largest Spanish-speaking country in the world?

Contestant: . . . Barcelona?

Host: I was actually after the name of a country . . .

Contestant: I'm sorry . . . I don't know the names of any other countries in Spain.

And, to be fair, such ignorance isn't restricted to local radio stations as it can rear its head on national radio just as easily:

From *The Steve Penk Breakfast Show*
(Virgin Radio)

Steve Penk: What is the name of the French-speaking Canadian state?
Contestant: America?

Penk: [starts to say something but is interrupted]
Contestant: Portugal? . . . Canada? [in increasingly shrill voice] Mexico? ITALY? SPAIN?

At the end of the day, maybe the problem is that some people just don't want to know about the world beyond their doorstep, as is beautifully summed up in this exchange from an American quiz show:

Host: This place is both a famous cathedral and a university.
Contestant: Pass.

Host: No, the answer was Notre-Dame.
Contestant: How am I supposed to know that? I'm from Indiana!

Speakers of English are notoriously resistant to learning other languages and even stubbornly resistant to learning the basics, as these moments, again from *The Weakest Link* (BBC), suggest:

Robinson: Which European language do the words 'Blitz', 'Kindergarten' and 'Angst' come from?
Contestant: Italian.

Robinson: Which country has the largest number of Portuguese speakers in the world?
Contestant: Spain.

Robinson: Mandarin and Cantonese are two languages that originated in which country?
Contestant: Spain.

Robinson: 'Achtung' is a word for warning in which European language?
Contestant: Chinese.

THE TROUBLE WITH CELEBRITIES AND TV

We live in a culture that is completely obsessed with celebrity and that means sometimes, when contest ants rake through their minds for information on, say, science or maths, they actually come up with a bizarre, completely wrong answer like Princess Diana or Tina Turner. Don't believe me? Read on:

From *Pointless* (BBC)

Alexander Armstrong: What member of the crow family, native to the UK, has a bare face.
Contestant: Russell Crowe?

Armstrong: The Asteroid 4238 Audrey is named after which actress?
Contestant: Kim Basinger.

Armstrong: Now then, Gemma, we want the names of these historical figures.

Gemma: [looking at board of questions] It's quite hard . . . I'm going to have to go with 'Assassinated by Lee Harvey Oswald in Dallas' as J.R. . . . but I think I might have gone completely wrong.

Armstrong: The wrong Dallas?

Gemma: [giggles] Yes.

Armstrong: J.R. . . . well . . . I really thought that was going to be a correct answer . . .

From *2CR* (FM)

Host: Who painted the ceiling of the Sistine Chapel?

Contestant: Leonardo DiCaprio.

From *Celebrity Squares* (ITV)

In this case the question is ludicrous from the start, but Burt Reynolds still manages to make things worse.

Host: What is that cute, small thing on Cher [audience laughter as Reynolds ponders the question], just below her waist?

Burt Reynolds: Sonny Bono.

From *Celebrity Name Game* (CBS)

Sheryl Crow: [attempting to give a clue so the contestant can identify Denzel Washington] His last name is our nation's capital.
Contestant: . . . Sacramento?

And given that the average person now spends five and a half hours a day watching TV and three hours a year reading a book (according to made-up statistics), it's not surprising that film and TV references come more naturally to many contestants than literary ones:

From *The Weakest Link* (BBC)

Robinson: Can you complete the title of the book by Jerome K. Jerome, *Three Men in a* . . . ?
Contestant: Baby.

One of the beauties of the next answer is that, by pure chance, the real answer isn't so far away from the popular version given by the contestant:

Robinson: William Burroughs' novel, first published in 1959, was *The Naked . . .* what?
Contestant: Chef?

Robinson: For which book did Salman Rushdie win the Booker prize?
Contestant: *The Wind in the Willows.*

* * *

HIGHBROW vs LOWBROW

Just occasionally contestants expecting a highbrow line of questioning are completely baffled when it comes to everyday lowbrow culture. The panic on the face of contestants from the London School of Economics and University College, Oxford, was a joy to behold when Jeremy Paxman asked the following three questions about an unidentified subject on *University Challenge* (BBC).

1. Which of the finalists shares a first name with Celia Johnson's character in the 1945 film *Brief Encounter*, and a surname with the first

England bowler to take 500 test wickets?

Following hushed consultation, the contestants passed on this one. Correct answer was Laura Andersen.

2. Josh Denzel's partner in third place has a first name closely resembling that of four kings of Poland. The third known as The Great reigned from 1333 to 1370. What is that contestant's first name?

This was also a pass; the contestants pulled agonised faces as they racked their brains for any remnants of medieval Polish history. The correct answer was Kazmir.

3. Wes shared fourth place with Megan Barton-Hanson. His surname is that of which paramour of Lady Emma Hamilton who died in battle in October 1805?

To the students' intense relief, while they still didn't know who 'Wes' was, they were able to work out that the answer was 'Nelson'.

At this point, Paxman revealed that the previously unidentified subject of the round was in fact the hugely popular reality dating show *Love Island*. As this show isn't thought to be intellectually stimulating, this revelation was greeted by extended laughter from the audience as the brainbox contestants' expressions veered between relief at the fact they hadn't been revealed as ignoramuses, condescending smirks at the very thought of *Love Island* being treated as a serious subject for their consideration and the gradually dawning suspicion that they were somehow being mocked by the audience.

* * *

CELEBRITY FAILS

We all know that being a celebrity doesn't a genius make you . . . but there can be a delicious pleasure in seeing famous faces sweating their way through horrendous quiz show performances.

For instance, in 2018 the American football star Rob Gronkowski appeared on *The $100,000 Pyramid* (ABC) alongside his teammate Julian Edelman. His quirky character was highlighted in the opening segment, when Edelman explained how he used to motivate Gronkowski: 'You know, sometimes everyone needs a little pick-me-up, so I used to say, "He's big, he's bad, he's a big, bad Gronk!"' Gronkowski immediately stood up, flexed his muscles and bizarrely roared like a lion at the audience. If they found that odd, they were going to find some of his later fails far more entertaining. Edelman was giving clues that the Gronk had to solve:

Julian Edelman: The sprinting African animal with the spots.
Rob Gronkowski: Tiger . . .

Edelman: The continent where the Nile runs?
Gronkowski: Egypt!

Edelman: No, the continent. Egypt is in . . . the big, old place . . .
Gronkowski: . . .

Edelman: [pointing at himself] I am a blank American.
Gronkowski: . . . [as buzzer goes] Africa!

When the roles were reversed, Gronkowski had to give Edelman a clue for a unicorn. The only rule he had to remember was that rhymes weren't allowed:

Gronkowski: It's one by itself . . . It's an animal . . . [makes pointy sign in front of nose]
Edelman: . . .

Gronkowski: [continues with his gesture]
Edelman: Rhinoceros?

Gronkowski: No . . . [looks stumped] . . . rhymes with 'porn'. . .
Edelman: Unicorn!

Happy Mondays singer Shaun Ryder's appearance on *Celebrity Mastermind* (BBC) was also a rich source of bizarre answers:

> **John Humphrys:** Bogota is the capital of which South American country?
> **Shaun Ryder:** Nigeria? [shrugs, unconcerned]

Ryder was also lost when he was asked of which self-governing island Stanley was the capital. After asking Humphreys to repeat the question, he misheard the word 'Stanley', the capital of the Falkland Islands, and answered 'Didn't he write Spiderman?'

Olympic taekwondo champion Jade Jones appeared on UK's boffin quiz *The Chase* (ITV), and unfortunately demonstrated how geographically challenged she was:

> **Bradley Walsh:** The film *Brave* is mainly set in which UK country?
> **Jade Jones:** [buzzes in and shouts] London!

The ex-model Jodie Marsh is now what is euphemistically referred to as a 'media personality', which means she tends to drift from one reality TV show to another without landing on what the rest of us call reality.

Anyhow, here's a nice moment from her appearance on BBC's *The Weakest Link*:

Anne Robinson: After Guernsey, Jersey and Alderney, what is the next largest of the Channel Islands?
Jodie Marsh: Ummm . . . is England a Channel Island?

And here's one from Montana Brown, a contestant in the 2018 *Love Island*, appearing on BBC's *Celebrity Mastermind* (which might be the ultimate oxymoron of a title):

John Humphrys: In what battle of October 1805 was a fleet commanded by Admiral Pierre-Charles Villeneuve defeated by a British fleet under the command of Lord Nelson?
Montana Brown: Hastings.

Our next big name appeared on the celebrity edition of the German show *Quiz Duel*. Bianca Heinicke, known in Germany as Bibi from her Youtube channel Bibi's Beauty Palace, was appearing with Julian, who also seems to be a YouTuber. Bibi has a strong following among young German girls, but has also received plenty of ridicule – a music video featuring her singing managed to rack up 3 million down-votes. So she was only inviting further ridicule with the following exchange:

> **Host:** What is something that, according to NASA scientists, most probably exists on Mars? [The options given were eco- and nuclear-generated electricity, flowing water, WiFi and underfloor heating].
> **Bibi:** Well, I have seen an ad for a villa on Mars that you can buy if you have enough money. So if there are houses on Mars there also has to be WiFi there . . .
>
> **Julian:** [muttering] That probably isn't right.
> **Bibi:** So the answer is . . . WiFi!

And now to Lydia Bright, star of reality show *The Only Way is Essex* (ITV; often referred to as 'TOWIE'). She thought she was on relatively safe ground having chosen the soft subject of the USA's *Sex and the City* (HBO) as her specialist subject. That probably just spurred the researchers on to try and trip her, which they comfortably succeeded in doing.

Her first question from Humphrys was 'Who was the only character – apart from Carrie, Miranda, Charlotte and Samantha – to appear in the pilot episode and series finale, *An American Girl in Paris: Part Deux*?' She wrongly answered, 'Skipper' (it's actually Mr Big. Doesn't absolutely everyone know that?).

Things went downhill when Humphrys upped the pedantry stakes on the next question, 'What is Steve's job when Miranda meets him in season 2?' Bright was given zero points because she accidentally said 'bar-attender' rather than 'bartender', which is a bit mean, but that's how the cookie crumbles. She did turn things round from there and managed to get a few correct answers on the subject of *Sex and the City*, but by then social media had already set off with a derogatory round of jokes about Essex girls. One (illiterate) Twitter user wrote, 'So Lydia is neither a celebrity or a mastermind and she certainly doesn't live up to her name'.

The British politician and former government minister David Lammy was another celebrity who was ridiculed after his appearance on the show. He rather set himself up for trouble by boasting in the preliminary chat with Humphrys that he had the 'gift of the gab', which he further defined as 'the ability to articulate something on behalf of a group of people who might not be able to articulate it themselves'. Here are a few of the highlights of his pretty poor performance, which might have made some of those poor, downtrodden people think twice about who they wanted to anoint as their spokesman:

John Humphrys: What is the married name of the scientist Marie Salomea Skłodowska who won the Nobel Prize for physics in 1903 for research into radiation?
David Lammy: Antoinette?

Humphrys: Curie. Cockpit Country is a rugged inaccessible area on which Caribbean island?
Lammy: Pass.

Humphrys: Jamaica. What was built to defend one of the gates of Paris and was later used as a state prison by Cardinal Richelieu?
Lammy: Versailles?

Humphrys: The Bastille. In February 2008, which Tottenham Hotspur player scored the first goal of Fabio Capello's reign as England football manager?
Lammy (who represents Tottenham in parliament): Aaron Lennon?

Humphrys: Jermaine Jenas. James Gandolfini played a mafia boss called Tony in which American television series?
Lammy: *The Godfather*?

Humphrys: *The Sopranos* . . . What name is used for the highest gallery of seats in a theatre?
Lammy: . . . Pass.

Lammy went on to fumble questions on MI5, the *News Quiz* (a well-known BBC radio programme on which many politicians appear), the name of the American military medal the Purple Heart and schoolboy chemistry. All of which went to demonstrate that the gift of the gab isn't much use to you when you are under the unforgiving lights of the *Mastermind* studio.

QUICKFIRE ROUND I

See if you can come up with better, or even funnier, answers

Q: The (UK) M4 motorway toll bridge crosses which river?
A: The Seine.

Q: What is 32 ÷ 8?
A: Six.

Q: In athletics, in which discipline does the competitor hold a metal ball under their chin before throwing it?
A: Discus.

Q: What name for an old British coin goes before 'fowl' and 'pig' to give two names of creatures?

A: Penny.

Q: A clog is worn on which part of the body?

A: The bottom.

Q: What was the principal language used by the ancient Romans?

A: Greek.

Q: Immediately before UK decimalization, there were how many shillings to a pound?

A: Three.

Q: What boy's name goes before 'snipe' and 'daw' to give two birds' names?

A: Peter.

Q: What 'X' is the fear of foreigners or strangers?
A: The X-Factor.

Q: What 'Mr-Man' is depicted as blue and covered in bandages?
A: Mr Accident.

Q: In the modern English alphabet, which is the penultimate letter?
A: Z.

Q: In the Second World War the word 'Commie' was a derogatory term for a person belonging to which political party?
A: Conservative.

Q: The wife of a marquess is known by which title?
A: Duchess.

Q: The road signs in the UK that warn drivers are of what geometric shape?
A: Z.

Q: A famous publisher of romantic novels was founded by Gerald Mills and Charles . . . what?
A: Dickens.

Q: What word can mean the touch-down of an aeroplane or the level floor between two staircases?
A: Step.

Q: A person who earns just enough for basic needs is said to live 'hand to . . .' what?
A: Foot.

Q: In the human body, what is the name of the main olfactory organ?
A: Liver.

Q: Cantaloupe, Galia and Honeydew are types of which fruit?
A: Orange.

AND NOW TO MONTY...

Panesar, the lovable, eccentric, ex-England cricketer whose career had varying levels of success. He had, on occasion, been known to buckle under the pressure of big occasions, but there were also other games in which the pressure made him take his game to new heights. So cricket fans were fascinated to see how he would perform on *Celebrity Mastermind* (BBC).

He started out reasonably well, scoring six points on his specialist subject, the history of the Sikh religion. He might have done better if he hadn't made the mistake of asking for one of the longer questions to be repeated. Sadly, the pressure of the lights, the occasion and John Humphrys' intimidating presence as question master seemed to finally get to him in the general knowledge round, in which he gave one of the programme's more bizarre, eccentric displays. Here's a post-match analysis of exactly what went wrong:

John Humphrys: How many pockets are there on a full-size snooker table?
Monty: Six.

A good positive start for Monty, a fast, short question promptly smacked to the boundary. Correct. So that should stand him in good stead for a strong total, right?

Humphrys: Which sign of the zodiac is represented by a crab?
Monty: Sagittar ... Scorpio!

This is an early sign of brain-freeze setting in, as Monty has started to give a kneejerk response to the trigger 'zodiac' before belatedly engaging his brain ... and still getting the answer wrong.

Humphrys: What is the title of A.A. Milne's stage adaptation of Kenneth Grahame's children's novel, *The Wind in the Willows*?
Monty: Harry Potter.

Oh dear, the pressure is starting to get to Monty. The relentless close-up shots of the *Mastermind* cameras show his eyes starting to dart around as he realizes he is in danger of rapidly losing his way:

Humphrys: Henry VIII had three wives called Catherine, two called Anne and another who died shortly after she gave birth to the future Edward VI. What was her name?
Monty: Elizabeth.

Let's be fair, this is the kind of trick often played in the trickier sorts of quiz shows as the initial information is irrelevant, and designed to derail your brain unless you truly concentrate on the actual question being asked. Still, wrong Monty. Wrong!

Humphrys: What is the standard international unit of absolute temperature; it is indicated by the letter 'K'?
Monty: Pass.

A sensible decision by Monty to leave this delivery without playing it. Perhaps he learned from the audience reaction of mixed shock and suppressed amusement to his awful 'Harry Potter' answer, but you can still see that the pressure is starting to get to him.

Humphrys: Which Asian island city state is served by Changi International Airport?
Monty: Shanghai.

First, as the question includes the words 'Asian' and 'city state', it's odds on that the answer is Singapore. But, more importantly, this kind of 'Echo Syndrome' is a classic sign of mental disintegration as the contestant simply says a word, any word, that sounds a bit like one of the words in the question. It's like a wild shot on goal from the halfway line in a soccer match; you might pull off a miracle but . . .

Humphrys: Birds described as 'pelagic' spend most of their lives flying over what?
Monty: The sky.

Later in the book I will talk about the temptation to call on Captain Obvious when the pressure is starting to get to you on a quiz show. This is a beautiful example as Monty mentally strips the question down to its simplest elements and answers a completely different question, 'Where do birds fly?' Wake up, man!

Humphrys: In what 1997 film do a group of unemployed men in Sheffield become strippers for a night at their local working men's club?
Monty: *The Dreamboys.*

And yes, The Dreamboys are a real group of male strippers. But the name of the hugely successful 1997 film contained a huge hint . . . his own name, *The Full Monty*. Oh, Monty, MONTY!

Humphrys: In which city is the Olympiastadion, built for the 1972 Olympics and where Germany's national football team played international matches until 2001?
Monty: Oh gosh . . . Athens?

This is the problem with the Captain Obvious approach: your brain sometimes strips out the words like 'Germany', which might at least have led Monty to guess something less silly. Instead his brain has only retained the absolute basic information 'city' and 'Olympics'.

Humphrys: What was the title of the first volume of C.S. Lewis's *Chronicles of Narnia* to be published; chronologically it follows *The Magician's Nephew*?
Monty: [sighs in desperation] C.J. Lewis?

And here is the 'Echo Syndrome' again, but that is NOW malfunctioning as say-anything Monty has simply, desperately tried to parrot the author's name, even getting that wrong.

Humphrys: Kimberlite, an igneous rock named after the South African city of Kimberley, is a rich source of what very precious stones?

Monty: Dunno . . . Pass.

Fair enough not to know this, but Monty's body language is now giving off terrible alarm calls of panic. Watching the programme again, you genuinely worry that he might, at any minute, simply stand up and run for the hills.

Humphrys: What were the Five Guys named in the title of the hit musical that was a tribute to the jazz bluesman, Louis Jordan?

Monty: Pass.

The question setters are almost taunting Monty, who was bizarrely referred to as 'Moe' at this point, while he just wants the pain to STOP.

Humphrys: In an 1819 poem, what season of the year does Keats describe as 'a season of mists and mellow fruitfulness'?

Monty: *Oliver Twist.*

OK, by this point even the viewer feels the best response might be to scream and run. Monty had a 25 per cent chance of getting the Keats question right if he just managed to retain the hint 'season' in his brain, but even that fleeting opportunity was missed. This is turning into a rout.

> **Humphrys:** In which city is the television comedy *Cheers* set?
> **Monty:** America.

CITY! NOT COUNTRY!! By now even John Humphrys' inscrutable expression is starting to crack. You can see he is willing Monty to just get one more question right, please God.

> **Humphrys** (last question): What national survey . . . [final buzzer sounds] . . . has been held in Britain every ten years since 1801, except for 1941 because of the Second World War?
> **Monty:** [doesn't even bother to try and answer, he is clearly just intensely relieved that his ordeal is over]

Monty did eventually see the funny side. Later, in interviews, he described how intimidating he had found the entire experience, and said he had intentionally taken a group of family and friends out to dinner on the night when it was broadcast so they wouldn't see it. Unfortunately, he realized during the meal that his name was trending on Twitter: a clip of his nightmare had gone viral. If he'd hoped it would be a flash in the pan, that hope was dashed when he got home and realized that he was the number one trending topic, while number two was *Oliver Twist*. His response? 'I switched my phone off and I threw it and went to sleep.' But he soon bounced back. 'I got up the next morning and watched the episode. Even I laughed at it. I can see why everyone's taking the piss, it was so funny.'

FUN WITH FORMATS

The clearer a show's format, the more you know things might go kaput. Let's start with the US *The Newlywed Game* (ABC), which began in 1966 and ran for eight and a half years, the longest-running daytime show until surpassed by *Family Feud* (CBS). You know the moment you put husbands and wives together (especially when they are still meant to be starstruck) all will most definitely NOT run smoothly.

There was a classic moment in the early days when the women were on stage alone and host Bob Eubanks asked, 'How many decades will your husband say his mother has lived?' One woman's response was 'ten decades' . . . well, OK. But when the men came out, the husband firstly admitted he didn't know what a decade was, so he laboriously worked through the maths, talking out loud. His mother was forty-four, and he figured a decade must be four years, so eventually he came up with . . . 'Ten decades?' More recent answers don't fail to raise a laugh either:

Q: What was the last Jewish food you ate?*
Wife 1: Chow mein.
Wife 2: Corn . . . [when her husband later chose bagels, she asked him what they are – his response, 'I don't know, I'm a Mormon']
Wife 3: I don't know . . . I haven't been Jewish in a long time.

* There are plenty of reasonable options that might be an answer to this question, like bagels, or matzos, for instance. But the wives on this show were a bit more creative in their view of Judaism.

Q: What is your favourite wind instrument?
A: Guitar.

Q: Who is your favourite classical composer?
Husband: Barry Manilow.
Wife: Elton John.

Q: What is your favourite thing to buy by the foot?
Wife: Shoes.

Bob: Shoes? You buy shoes by the foot?

Q: What is your favourite crustacean?
Wife: The stuff that gets in your eyes when you sleep.
Husband: Lobster.
Wife: [when she hears her husband's answer] Isn't crust stuff that gets in your eyes when you sleep? That's not a lobster!

Q: What is your least favourite fowl?
Husband: Sauerkraut.

Q: How many showers did your wife take on her wedding day?
Husband: She doesn't take showers, she takes baths.

Q: What's your husband's favourite condiment?
Wife 1: Pool table.
Wife 2: Karate School.

Q: What is your favourite pasta?
Husband: Flat on my stomach, looking at the TV screen [he misheard 'pasta' as 'posture'].

Q: What would your husband say is his very favourite kind of rodent?
Wife: I don't know what a rodent is . . . his saxophone?

Q: What will your wife say is her favourite giblet?
Husband: Her panties.

Q: My wife and I prefer to keep the inside of our refrigerator at (blank) degrees.
Husband: 200 degrees

A TV format can spark further problems, especially when you involve celebrities; they barely even seem to know what show they are on, as though their agent has witlessly accepted an invitation for them to appear without pointing out that a faint familiarity with the rules might actually help. A great example comes from *EastEnders* actor Nitin Gattara's appearance on *Pointless* (both BBC).

If you haven't seen the show, the main hook is an inversion of the *Family Fortunes/Family Feud* (ITV/CBS) round because contestants have to guess the correct answers to questions as given by the fewest number of individuals in a survey (hence the aim to be pointless and increase the jackpot). So, if the question is name winners of three or more acting Oscars, you might find that plenty of people obviously name Katharine Hepburn, Daniel Day-Lewis, Meryl Streep and Jack Nicholson (all giving a high score), while Ingrid Bergman would be a less obvious choice and Walter Brennan – who also achieved the same feat (winning three Academy Awards in 1936, 1938 and 1940) – even less so, giving a desired low score.

Nitin's ordeal started when he was confronted with a board with options for the game of *Monopoly* including categories such as Stations and Streets. He confidently plumped for Stations and stood back waiting for Alexander Armstrong to ask a question. Armstrong, always urbane and calm, patiently explained that he was supposed to pick a station that might be pointless.

So while the panic station in Nitin's mind started to grind slowly into gear, he pondered the problem for a while and blurted out 'Bounds Green', which is a relatively obscure London underground station, but it is certainly not one of the stations on the *Monopoly* board for London. Whereupon:

Alexander Armstrong: Now, OK, we're gonna go back a couple of spaces . . . [patiently explains the rules] Yes . . . so now, you know, you're fully in possession of the facts.

Nitin Gattara: [stares vacantly at screen of options] Out of those . . . I'm really lost here.

Rita Simons [Nitin's teammate and co-star on *EastEnders*]: Just say something.

Gattara: OK . . . I'll say anything. . . yeah something, it's gonna be a space on the Monopoly board but it's going to be . . .

Armstrong: Right it's going to be a space on the Monopoly board.

Gattara: OK . . . so it would be the name of something on the Monopoly board . . . right [a distant light finally appears in his eyes, but he is obviously worried it might just be another train coming down the tunnel towards him], I couldn't say 'Go To Jail', could I?

Armstrong: Yes! [extended audience applause]
Gattara: Thank ****ing ***** for that!

Alexander: Yes . . . that's we were all thinking.

The best that can be said for the rest of Nitin's appearance on the show is that he managed to deal with his total lack of understanding of the format with charming grace, and at least managed to come across as a decent human being, if not a decent *Pointless* contestant.

* * *

STRIP POKER

And talking of formats . . . One particularly ridiculous 1990s quiz show from the US was *Strip Poker* (USA Broadcasting), in which two male and two female contestants sat around a table while the host asked questions. When a contestant got a question wrong they removed an item of clothing. The teaser was that someone might end up naked, though the closest anyone actually got to this was revealing a layer of beachwear under their clothes. The suggestive idiocy of the questions, and the fact that the contestants were clearly selected for their looks rather than their brains, meant it was inevitable that there would be some prize bits of stupidity in the answers:

Host: What is the hardest substance on Earth?
Contestant: Water.

Host: By what feline name do Kate Moss and her model friends refer to the runway?
Contestant: Fork.
Host: Pigs ruled the world in the novel *Animal Farm*. Who wrote it?
Contestant: Stuart Little?

Host: Your boyfriend has fantasies involving Anna Kournikova and her friends playing with balls. What sport does Anna Kournikova play professionally?
Contestant: Juggling?
Question: True or false? *Chock Full o' Nuts* is a brand of coffee?
Contestant: [Looks blank] . . . Mocha?
Host: You're watching sugarplum fairies dancing on the stage. What ballet has your girlfriend dragged you to?
Contestant: Aerobics?

* * *

GOLDEN GOGAN

Larry Gogan was a legendary Irish DJ who hosted *The Golden Hour* (RTÉ 2) for four decades, and for most of that time the show featured his just-a-minute quiz. One of his catchphrases was his warm, understanding response when contestants did especially badly, and he would reassure them by saying, 'Sure, they didn't really suit you'.

In an interview he once said, 'Well, regarding the catchphrase, I hear that everywhere I go. It's the first thing people say to me! But, I feel that you have to be fair to people, especially if they don't do well.' The interviewer then asked if he understood why people sometimes failed so spectacularly and answered, 'Not really. I'd say that nerves must play a part if someone doesn't do well. But I wouldn't be into slagging people off.'

The quiz was the source of many well-known bloopers, some of which are only really funny if you have a good knowledge of Irish culture. So, to the February 2006 question 'What famous star is followed by travellers?' came the answer 'Joe Dolan' – a cheesy Irish showbiz mainstay, best known as Boots and for his association with showbands. Fortunately, one widely circulated email lists the following bloopers from the just-a-minute quiz (and yes, some can be found in other quiz show fails):

Larry Gogan: Name something a blind man might use.
Caller: A sword.

Gogan: Name a song with the word 'moon' in the title.
Caller: 'Blue Suede Moon'.

Gogan: What is Hitler's first name?
Caller: Heil.

Gogan: Name the capital of France.
Caller: F.

Gogan: Name a bird with a long neck.
Caller: Naomi Campbell.

Gogan: Name an occupation where you might need a torch.
Caller: A burglar.

Gogan: Where is the Taj Mahal?
Caller: Opposite the Dental Hospital.

Gogan: Name something that floats in a bath.
Caller: Water.

Gogan: Name some famous brothers.
Caller: Bonnie and Clyde.

Gogan: Name a dangerous race.
Caller: The Arabs.

Gogan: Name a famous Royal.
Caller: Mail.

Gogan: Name an item of clothing worn by the Three Musketeers.
Caller: A horse.

Gogan: Name something you wear on a beach.
Caller: A deckchair.

Gogan: Name a famous bridge.
Caller: 'The Bridge Over Troubled Waters'.

Gogan: Name something a cat does.
Caller: Goes to the toilet.

Gogan: Name something you do in the bathroom.
Caller: Decorate.

Gogan: Name a sign of the Zodiac.
Caller: April.

Gogan: Name a method of securing your home.
Caller: Put the kettle on.

Gogan: Name something associated with pigs.
Caller: The police.

Gogan: Name something you do before you
go to bed.
Caller: Sleep.

Gogan: Name something people might be
allergic to.
Caller: Skiing.

Gogan: Name something you put on walls.
Caller: A roof.

Gogan: Name something slippery.
Caller: A conman.

Gogan: Name a kind of ache.
Caller: A fillet of fish.

Gogan: Name a jacket potato topping.
Caller: Jam.

Gogan: Name a mint named after a Grand Prix commentator.*
Contestant: . . .

Gogan: 'You suck them . . .'
Contestant: 'Dickie Davis'.

* The answer was Murray Walker.

Gogan: Name a famous Scotsman.
Caller: Jock . . .? Vinnie Jones!

Gogan: Something you open, other than a door.
Caller: Your bowels.

We've followed tradition, listing this anecdote under Gogan, but it actually comes from *Family Fortunes* (ITV).

Gogan: Name a food that can be brown or white
Caller: A potato.

Gogan: Name something that flies that doesn't have an engine.
Caller: A bicycle with wings.

Gogan: Complete this phrase: 'As happy as . . .'
Contestant: Errmm . . .

Gogan: Think of me when you're answering.
Contestant: A pig in sh**e.

In the same interview mentioned earlier, Larry was specifically asked about this list. His answer: 'Now, they're not true at all! I'm nearly certain of that. I even know where that one, the one about "A pig in sh**e", where that came from. It was a joke Brendan Grace used to have in his act. Someone heard it one night and then told it on Gay Byrne's show . . . To this day, people come up to me and say, "Oh I was listening that day when you asked the 'As happy as. . .' question!" and sure it never happened at all!'

So, here's confirmation that at least some of these bloopers are actually very Irish inventions. In addition, at least two of the items (the Naomi Campbell and bowels) actually come from the UK quiz show *Family Fortunes* (ITV), suggesting that there may be a few more which have been misattributed or even invented.

When compiling a book of this sort, you always need to be aware that some apparently real bloopers may not have actually occurred, but it only takes one source to say that it really did for others to pick it up and run with it. And after a while the bloopers' origins are completely lost. So, I've used original recordings wherever possible, but I can't put my hand on heart and claim there aren't a few more misattributions in this book.

When it comes to the Larry Gogan just-a-minute quiz bloopers, let's hang on to that 'nearly certain' and accept that, while not every fail on the list is a true story, some of them undoubtedly are . . . and the ones that aren't really should be!

THE *BLOCKBUSTERS* CHRONICLES AND GOLDEN OLDIES

Blockbusters in both the UK and US (ITV, then on various channels; NBC) was a cheesy afternoon quiz show in which the contestants had to make their way across a board by answering questions that were generated by a capital letter. Sometimes the questions were a bit tricksy, with a twist designed to fool contestants into answering too fast. For instance, original UK host Bob Holness once started by asking, 'What "J" sits in a box . . . ?', at which point a contestant pressed her buzzer and snapped back 'Jack'. Bob then completed the question, 'What "J" sits in a box . . . and decides on the outcome of a court case?' The unfortunate contestant still got the answer wrong, going for 'judge' rather than 'jury', but never mind.

Some of the humour in the UK version came from Bob's erratic responses; sometimes he came across as a home counties bully, at other times being urbane and the definition of professionalism. The result was a pretty low-budget affair that occasionally teetered close to hysteria:

Bob: What 'O' is the generic word for any living animal or plant, including bacteria and viruses?

Contestant: Orgasm [suddenly looks mortified and panicky; the correct answer was organism].

Bob: There are reasons [he's as calm and unruffled as ever] that I won't go into why I cannot accept that answer.

Bob: What 'L' is a sum of money you borrow from a bank?

Contestant: Can I have a loan, please, Bob?

Bob: [says nothing, but takes his wallet out and walks over to her]

Bob: What 'L' do you make in the dark when you're making a wild guess?

Contestant: Love?

Bob: What 'W' are made from plastic or card for carrying papers, and from leather for . . . [contestant buzzes in but does not speak].

Bob: Yes [and then supplies the answer, wallet [at which point both Bob and the contestant look confused].

On another occasion, the correct answer to a question relating to London was 'parks'. The expression on Bob's face teetered between professionalism and disaster when the contestant gave the answer 'prostitutes'.

Bob: What 'N' is meant by the phrase, 'Hit him on the Boko?'
Contestant: Nob.
Second Contestant: . . . Nag?

Bob: . . .

Bob: What 'K' is a suicide mission for a pilot?
Contestant: Kama Sutra.

The next one is not so much a fail, as a spectacular example of an erudite quiz show question:

Bob: What 'C' has four stiff-standers, four dilly-danders, two lookers, two crookers and a wig-wag?*

* The actual answer should have been 'cow' (the above terms mean 'four legs, four teats, two eyes, two horns and a tail'). Unsurprisingly, the contestants were stumped.

I mentioned that some of the questions were intentionally tricksy. This example comes from the head-to-head round, in which you could buzz in to get an advantage by answering the question early:

Bob: So, what word beginning in 'D' describes any camel that . . .
Contestant 1: [buzzes in looking super confident] It's a dromedary camel, Bob.

Bob: Sorry, that's incorrect and the question goes to your opponent. What word beginning in 'D' describes any camel that isn't alive anymore?
Contestant 2: Dead!

As you can see, there are plenty of funny quiz show answers that though dating back decades, still turn up in the tabloids and social media lists. While some of them may be familiar, they are still a hoot. This batch of Q's and A's all come from *Family Feud* (CBS):

Q: During what month of pregnancy does a woman begin to look pregnant?
Answer: September.

Q: Using the barter system, what is something you would trade your husband for?
A: Bread.

Q: Name a scary animal.
A: A squirrel.

Q: Name a yellow fruit.
A: Orange.

Q: Name something you feel before you buy it.
A: Excited.

Q: Name a type of bear.
A: Papa bear.

Q: Name a man's name that starts with the letter 'K'.
A: Kentucky Fried Chicken.

Q: Name an animal that can be spelled with three letters.
A: Alligator.

Q: Name something Russia is famous for.
A: Rus.

And from the Canadian version of the same show:

Q: What is Popeye's favourite food?
A: Chicken!

From *The Match Game* (ABC)

Q: My new restaurant chain is so bad, when I open a new location, a (blank) opens next door.*
A: Massage parlour.

* All six panellists on the show had the same guess written on their cards – 'Hospital'.

Q: While walking down the beach, I found a message in a bottle. The message said, 'I'm trapped on a deserted island with Scarlett Johansson. Please send (blank).'
A: Hair [following booing from the audience, panellist Alec Baldwin demanded an explanation for this answer, invoking 'a clause in my contract' to justify this. The contestant responded, 'She has amazing hair . . .']

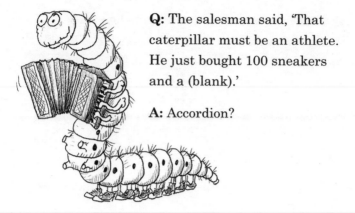

Q: The salesman said, 'That caterpillar must be an athlete. He just bought 100 sneakers and a (blank).'

A: Accordion?

Q: Candied (blank).

[In this case the humour comes from the audience response to the question: two of the top three answers chosen by the audience were 'apples' and 'yams', both of which are indeed often to be found candied in the US. However, the second most popular answer was 'Camera'.]

Q: Bart (blank).
A: [after much deliberation] Black?

[To make this worse, one of the members of the panel was Marcia Wallace who is the voice of teacher Mrs Krabappel on *The Simpsons*, a surname that surely would have provided the more obvious answer.]

Q: (Blank) wrench.
A: Nut wrench!

Q: Instead of receiving Egg Foo Yung, Ollie received Egg Foo (blank).
A: Mein?

Q: Dumb Donald is so dumb, he bought a new Volkswagen Rabbit and filled it with (blank).*
A: Wine.

Q: What would be your second choice?
A: Milk.

Q: 'Rabbit,' I said. I really tried to lean on that as hard as I could. Now, think, what would be your third choice?
A: I don't know, I don't have a third choice.

* The panellists all chose things rabbit eat: lettuce, cabbage and pellet food.

Q: Dwayne Johnson has agreed to fight Justin Bieber at the next WrestleMania. They're billing it as 'The Rock vs. The (blank)'.
A: Pillow.

Q: I think my doctor is a quack. He replaced my heart with a cow's. Now people are trying to (blank) me.

A: Eat.

Q: Last Friday was Single's Night at Chuck E. Cheese. To heat things up, they filled the ball pit with (blank).

A: Fish [he had misheard it as 'Seagull's Night', though what that might be nobody knows].

Q: Out of Touch Orville was so out of touch, he thought electronic dance music was two (blanks) doing the tango.

A: . . . Electrical cords?

QUICKFIRE ROUND II

See if you can come up with better, or even funnier, answers

Q: The phrase much used by football pundits is 'early windows' or 'early doors'?
A: Early windows.

Q: Who became US president when Nixon resigned?
A: Kennedy.

Q: The ancient site known as the Valley of the Kings is in which country?
A: England.

Q: The nickname of the Duke of Wellington included which metallic element?
A: Fire.

Q: William the Conqueror was the first king of which Royal House?
A: Windsor.

Q: What is 21 + 79?
A: 98.

Q: What war-time song by Vera Lynn included the words 'Don't know where, don't know when?'
A: We'll come again.

Q: The word 'ape' is an anagram of which small vegetable?
A: Apple.

Q: What letter in the modern alphabet lies between P and R?
A: O.

Q: What name for someone qualified to fly a plane precedes 'fish' and 'whale' to give the names of two sea creatures?
A: Shell.

Q: What 'T' is the answer to any addition sum?
A: Takeaway.

Q: Emperor Augustus used to boast that in Rome he had found a city made of brick and left it made of what stone?
A: Rubble.

Q: In childhood, an outdoor meal with soft stuffed toys is known by what three-word name?
A: Humpty Dumpty.

Q: Cotton buds carry a warning not to insert them into which part of the body?
A: Eyes.

Q: A book about the stereotype of male masculinity is entitled *Real Men Don't Eat* . . . what?
A: Food.

Q: What is 333 ÷ 3?
A: 21.

Q: The Johnny Cash song was called 'A Boy Named . . .' what?
A: Joe.

Q: What is 358 − 357?
A: 4.

Q: What is 12 + 13?
A: 35.

NAME SOMETHING THAT...

Any quiz that asks open-ended questions such as 'Name something that has eight legs' is inviting idiotic answers such as 'two horses'. Of course, the aim of the round in *Family Fortunes* (ITV) in which the host asks such questions is for the contestant to try to give one of the most popular answers previously given by a panel. The UK version of the show tends not to be as risqué as the US version *Family Feud* (CBS), so you would expect contestants to play it safe and come up with something obvious, but when the lights are on and the heart is racing, some peculiar answers do burst out of people's mouths:

Host: Name a famous robber.
Contestant: Cops.

Host: Any part of the body beginning with the letter 'N'.
Contestant: Name?

Host: Name something you wouldn't try even once.

Contestant: Sex on a train.

Host: Something a dentist says.

Contestant: Just a small prick.

Host: Something a car can have two of.

Contestant: Wheels.

Host: Isn't that called a bike?

Host: Slang word for money.

Contestant [who is a sweet, old lady]: Bitch.

Host: Bitch? No, not Mummy. . . Money!

Host: Something people have more than two of on their body.

Contestant: Arms

Host: [steps back to examine contestant] You've got more than two, have you?

Host: Something that comes in sevens.

Contestant: Fingers.

Host: [counts his own fingers ostentatiously, then leans over to examine contestant's hands]

Host: Something everyone has only one of.

Contestant: Big toe.

Host: A place where you would keep a pen.

Contestant: Zoo.

Host: Something you associate with the sea.

Contestant one: Deckchairs.

Contestant two: Coffin.

Host: Coffee???

Contestant two: Coffin . . .

Host: You get very ill at sea do you? Oh, you're thinking of the letter 'C' . . . SEA, I meant.

Host: Something a girl should know about a man before she marries him.

Contestant: His name.

Host: Something that people close.
Contestant (a young, female): Legs.

Host: [looks at camera and does a double take]

Host: A place you wouldn't expect to meet a nun.
Contestant: A brothel.

Host: Something you would jump on and ride.
Contestant: [hesitates and gives a sly smile] Your partner.

Host: A way of toasting someone.
Contestant: Over a fire [cue audience laughter, and the contestant puts hand over mouth and looks embarrassed].

Host: I tell you what, if it's up there, I'll give you the money myself [they go to the answer board and 'Grill' lights up as the answer given by 12 per cent of those asked].

Host: Oh no . . . I owe you [looks at scoreboard] £12!

As I said, the open-ended questions on *Family Feud* the US, CBS version of *Family Fortunes*, tend to be more risqué, to the point where it is pretty clear that the producers are egging contestants on to say something incriminating or rude in front of their families. The result is some pretty comical moments, often emphasized by host Steve Harvey's tendency to mug and talk to the camera and audience.

Steve Harvey: We asked 100 married men . . . Fantasy only, fantasy only . . . What would you do the first day after being divorced?
Contestant one: Threesome [when they go to the board, '*Ménage à trois*' is actually the second-placed answer with 17 per cent!]
Contestant two: [buzzer cuts him off].

Harvey: [to audience] Let me tell you something . . . Pete's a married man. Pete said, 'I'm not saying a damn thing'! You're a smart man, Pete.

Harvey: We asked 100 married men . . . Name something your ex-girlfriend was better at than your wife.
Contestant: Oral sex . . . [camera cuts to his wife with an expression that could be amused or aghast, then cuts back to contestant slowly looking over his shoulder to see how she is reacting].

Harvey: [looks straight at camera with a deadpan face] 'You happy?' [turns to contestant] 'You're damn stupid . . .' [turns to answer board and points

to the top answer, with 38 per cent, which is indeed
'Romancing the bone'].

Harvey: Between us, tell us something about a
chicken that reminds you of your wife.
Contestant one: They both hatch [gets no points].
Contestant two: They lay eggs [ditto, nil points].
Contestant three: They 'cock-a-doodle-doo? [in
spite of Harvey's sceptical expression and audience
derision, the top answer, with 40 per cent, is indeed
'cackles/clucks'].

Harvey: We asked 100 married men, name a button
on the remote you wish worked on your wife.
Contestant: Power.
Contestant two: Mute [both get points on the
answer board].

Harvey: We asked 100 married women if you could
change one part of your husband's body what would
it be?
Contestant (a married woman): His penis . . . I
know, I know, I come from a weird place . . . You
were thinking it.

Harvey: I wasn't thinking a damn thing. That's
your husband over there. He's having a bad day.

Harvey: Something with a motor that's a necessity.
Contestant: I'm going to say vibrator, Steve.

Harvey: 'I'd walk around the house nude if I didn't have . . .'
Contestant: Expensive furniture.

Harvey: Something a divorced man hopes his ex-wife would do.*
Contestant (who is standing next to his wife): [muttering quietly] . . . sorry for this . . . [then much louder, in angry voice] DIE!

Harvey: [leans in and gives him an over-the-top high five]
Contestant's wife: [turns angrily towards her husband]
Contestant: [defensively] We're not divorced!
Contestant's wife: [exchanges high five with her husband and hugs him]

* The number one answer is 'die/get eaten by hyenas'.

* * *

WHEN HOSTS FAIL

Steve Harvey is well known for his gaffes and misunderstandings with contestants. On one show a contestant was asked to guess reasons women might give for breaking up with a boyfriend.

Contestant: He spent all my money . . .
Harvey: [walking off looking befuddled] 'He ate spaghetti on a Monday'?

* * *

SO WRONG THEY'RE ALMOST RIGHT

Often wrong answers given by contestants are plain wrong, and don't provide much amusement or en-lightenment beyond revealing the ignorance or brain freeze of the contestant. For instance, when Eamonn Holmes on the *National Lottery Show* (BBC) asked the contestant to name the largest country in South America and got the answer 'Nairobi', there is not much more to be said. By contrast, there are times when contestants on game shows come up with an-swers so bizarre that they have a certain poetry, a mad inspiration. For instance:

From *Family Feud* (CBS)

Host: What might a blind date conveniently forget to mention about himself?
Female Contestant: [as if this would be obvious to anyone with common sense] He's blind!

From *Tipping Point* (ITV)

Ben Shephard: What date is Christmas Day traditionally celebrated in the UK?
Contestant: Wednesday.

Shephard: In 1987, which infamous headland in the east of Cornwall was bought for nearly £7 million by the property tycoon Peter De Savary?
Contestant: The London Eye.

From *Pointless* (BBC)

Alexander Armstrong: Complete the popular saying, 'Always a bridesmaid, never the . . .'
Contestant: Groom?

From *The Vault* (ITV)

Melanie Sykes: What is the name given to the condition where the sufferer can fall asleep at any time?
Contestant: Nostalgia.

While this contestant on *The Chase* (ITV) seems to have spent too much time watching sci-fi movies and not enough looking at maps:

Bradley Walsh: Name the only known inhabited planet in the universe.
Contestant: Mars.

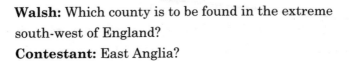

Walsh: Which county is to be found in the extreme south-west of England?
Contestant: East Anglia?

Meanwhile, the answer given by this contestant on *Steve Wright in the Afternoon* (BBC Radio) is so beautiful that it should probably be officially adopted into the Italian language:

Steve Wright: What is the Italian word for motorway?
Contestant: . . . Expresso.

Incidentally, a similarly beautiful bit of naming occurred in BBC's *Mastermind* when a contestant was challenged to name the English equivalent of the Spanish *autopista* and the German *autobahn* and answered, 'pistachio'.

From *Fighting Fitz* (BBC Radio Devon)

David Fitzgerald: In Canada, there is a city called London. What river does it lie on?
Caller: [pauses] The Danube.

e (ABC) with Bob Eubanks, the wives
dies, from your living room window,
would you say the sun comes up every
often.' One answer was, 'Well, Bob,
room faces west . . . so, um, north?'
the obvious answer – the sun rises in
less of the view from your living room.
, there are situations in which the
question is so wrong it's right, as this
moment shows:

mstrong: We asked 100 people
ny of *The Dirty Dozen* and *The*
ven actors as they could. Now . . .
'll take a very random guess and go
Brown.

hesitates, with sardonic face] That
en fun . . . Yeah that's what it
soundtrack, definitely [he turns to
adds, sarcastically] JAMES BROWN
that's right . . . let's see how many
. . there is your red line [the line
nd, indicating that the answer is
t]. What? OMG. [the line continues
the way to zero, giving a perfect score
e of those asked in a survey came up
er]

puts hands in the air triumphantly]

From *Mastermind* (BBC)

John Humphrys: Napoli is the Italian name for
which city?
Contestant: Milan.

Now, has your spelling ever let you down at a key
moment? From *Wheel of Fortune* (CBS), bear in mind
you can choose either a letter to fill in the gaps or
to guess the whole phrase. One contestant was faced
with this board:

E_CLUSIVE NIGHTCLUB

And do you know what they answered? 'I'll take a "K"!

Host: There are some street names common to
cities all over the US. Name one.
Contestant: Hollywood Boulevard.

From *The Weakest Link* (BBC)

Anne Robinson: In travel . . . British traffic lights
are green, amber and . . . ?
Contestant: Green.

Robinson: Name the long-running TV comedy show about pensioners, *Last of the . . .* what?
Contestant: Mohicans.

Robinson: What is the name of the cord cut after a woman gives birth?
Contestant: Biblical cord.

Robinson: How many wheels does a unicycle have?
Contestant: Two.

From *Master*

John Humpl
Napoleon put
October 1795
Contestant:

From *The Ch*
Walsh: A £2 c
a schoolboy er
what? A swor
Contestant:

From *The Na*
Eamonn Hol
matter: solid,
Contestant:

Wheel of Fortu
where guests h
ing?') from a fe
umbrella, a coc
guessed 'Idaho'
ment because o
audience and p

And you h
sometimes, esp
signed to make

Newlywed Gar
were asked, 'I
what direction
morning, most
well, our livin
No one noticed
the east regar

And finall
answer to the
Pointless (BBC

Alexander A
to name as m
Magnificent S
Contestant:
for . . . James

Armstrong:
would have b
needed, a fun
the board and
. . . let's see if
people said it
starts to desc
actually corre
to descend all
because not o
with this ans

Contestant:

Armstrong: I've seen some luck in my time on this show . . .

Contestant: [takes a bow to the audience, sharing the joke]

Richard Osman [the adjudicator]: I mean the soul legend wasn't in the film but there's an old American actor called Jim Brown . . . His real name is James Samuel Brown and he WAS in *The Dirty Dozen*!

SO CLOSE, YET SO FAR...

If quiz shows are partly enjoyable because of the *schadenfreude* in watching a contestant failing to answer the simplest question, this is only intensified when you can see the contestant panicking, clearly closing in on the answer but STILL unable to find the right words. Or when they embarrass themselves with an answer that is just hopelessly inappropriate, like the *Dog Eat Dog* (BBC) contestant who, on being asked by Ulrika Jonsson to name the German national airline answered, 'The Luftwaffe'.

From *The Chase* (ITV)

Bradley Walsh: Name the television naturalist the Attenboroasaurus dinosaur is named after.

Answer: Errr, Atten . . . boro. . . . . pass.

From *Family Feud* (CBS)

Host: Real or fictional, name a famous Willy.
Contestant: Willy the Pooh.

From *Wheel of Fortune* (CBS)

Contestants have to guess a well-known phrase or sentence for which the letters are revealed, one by one. Following a particularly useless series of guesses, the two contestants were faced with this:

**DOPEY, GRUMPY, DOC, BASHFUL,
HAPPY, SNEE_Y AND SLEEPY**

Contestant one: Sneeky!

Another contestant had the following letters and had to guess the phrase:

MAGIC _AND

Contestant: Magic Hand, Magic Band . . . Magic . . . [starts to gabble in panic] Tand, Band, Sand . . . Dand, Fand, Sand, Cand . . . [buzzer cuts him off] Wand! [explaining to host] Oh, man . . . That 'and' looked so . . . 'and . . . y'.

And now for some more what-IS-wrong-with-you? moments:

From *Daryl Denham's Drivetime*
(BBC Radio Oxford)

Daryl Denham: In which country would you spend shekels?
Contestant: Holland?

Denham: Try the next letter of the alphabet.
Contestant: Iceland? Ireland?

Denham: [helpfully] It's a bad line. Did you say Israel?
Contestant: No.

From *Pointless* (BBC)

Alexander Armstrong: What's the only stroke in the swimming medley that doesn't begin with the letter B?
Contestant: Breaststroke.

From *Celebrity Name Game* (CBS)

For the final question, which would decide the eventual prize-winner, Craig Ferguson had been trying to give contestants hints about the character Odie (Garfield's canine friend) in the Garfield movies:

Craig Ferguson: It starts with the letter 'O' . . . it sounds like that and the fourth letter of the alphabet . . .
Contestants: [blank faces]

Ferguson: If I took a great deal of heroin, I would probably . . . ?

Contestants: [buzzing in] Overdose.

Ferguson: [losing his rag and shouting] The answer was 'Odie'. O!!! D!!!

From *Steve Wright in the Afternoon* (BBC Radio)

Steve Wright: What is the capital of Australia?
Contestant: . . .

Wright: And it's not Sydney.
Contestant: . . . Sydney?

From *The Paul Wappat Show*
(BBC Radio Newcastle)

Paul Wappat: How long did the Six-Day War between Egypt and Israel last?
Contestant: [excruciating pause] Fourteen days?

From *This Morning with Richard and Judy* (ITV)

Host: The Berlin Wall was demolished in which country?
Contestant: Erm . . .

Host: East and West came together . . .
Contestant: . . .
Host: It begins with a 'G'.
Contestant: Er . . .
Host: No, I can't give you that one.

From *The Weakest Link* (BBC)

Robinson: In which century was Hadrian's Wall built?

Contestant: The eighteenth century.

From LBC Radio

Host: What name does Cat Stevens go under now?

Contestant: . . .

Host: I'll give you a clue, he became a Muslim.

Contestant: Abu Hamza?

* * *

THE GOLD STAR FOR 'WHAT HAVE I SAID?'

Sometimes it's worth having a bit of sympathy for the devil. Or at least for the hapless quiz show contestant whose idiotic answers go viral and continue to embarrass them long after the original gaffe. In 2018, Evan Kaufman was on the American show *The $100,000 Pyramid* (originally CBS).

For the last round of the game Kaufman was paired up with the *Saturday Night Live* actor Tim Meadows, and had to give him a clue that would lead to the correct answer. When given 'People whose last name is Obama', his first response was 'Bin Laden'. Of course, echoing the mindless anti-Obama rhetoric of internet trolls was the last thing he had intended, but the clip was immediately copied to social media sites and he became notorious as the 'Racist Game Show Guy'. What wasn't shown was Kaufman's immediate realization of his error and attempt to self-correct. Which didn't help his cause.

Bravely, he took to social media afterwards to give his side of the story: apart from being exhausted (as he had a two-week-old baby) and somewhat starstruck in the company of Meadows, he also got himself into a mental tangle after producers banged it into his head that the answers in the final round weren't obvious and to make sure he read the question carefully.

He described the awful moment: 'I read "People whose last name is Obama". I freeze. There's only one. BARACK OBAMA. The man I would have voted for three times! . . . And so you have this perfectly viral clip. A clip that is insanely funny. It would be so funny if it wasn't me. But this just goes to show you that even a liberal "Globalist Cuck" like yours truly has some inherent racism lurking in my brain. What a disaster.'

He'd hoped that the producers would be kind enough to edit the moment out and spare his blushes: some hope . . .

* * *

WHO ISN'T GOING TO BE A MILLIONAIRE? I

On the hugely successful quiz show *Who Wants to Be a Millionaire?* (originally ITV before going multinational), the initial questions are intentionally so easy that it is more or less impossible for the contestants to fail and not pocket the first few thousand dollars or pounds. However, never underestimate the ability of human beings to give bizarre answers under pressure. Let's start with a contestant who compounded his embarrassment with a bombastic opening speech:

Contestant: I tell you what, I remember watching *Millionaire* as a little kid . . . and it was such a phenomenon, tens of millions of people watching a show about smart people every night, celebrating being smart and I thought, you know what, maybe it's not so bad being smart, maybe it's not bad being a nerd, maybe it's cool to be smart and I followed that all the way and I just graduated from medical school.

Host: Congratulations, that's awesome. Maybe some lingering bills from med. school to be paid off?
Contestant: Perhaps.

Host: Let's take care of that today.
Contestant: Let's work on it.

Host: [explains the rules] Ready to go . . . Are you ready?
Contestant: [super-confidently] I'm always ready.

Host: Without further ado, let's play *Who Wants to Be a Millionaire?* Here's your $500 question. Snapping selfies in kitchens you can't afford and taking a meatball break are two things Buzzfeed says every twenty-something should do on their first trip . . .

    (a) to Paris

    (b) London

    (c) Rome or

    (d) IKEA.

Contestant: [clearly overthinking the question and speaking briskly] I tell you what, I think they do serve meatballs in IKEA, and err . . . I don't think that's the answer though. So, meatballs . . . sounds like Rome to me. In fact, if I won a million dollars, I'd love to take a trip to Italy. So I'm going to say Rome, final answer.

Host: Brent . . . It was IKEA . . . IT WAS IKEA! Oh no . . . Oh nooo . . .

Contestant: [falls forward with head in hands before being consoled and ushered off by host]

Host: What is a pecan?

(a) Root vegetable

(b) Type of nut

(c) Cut of beef

(d) Tropical bird.

Contestant: Pecan? Type of nut . . . I like nuts. Pecan. Root vegetables, I don't do a lot of that. I do like beef. Pecan? Tropical bird . . . Yes, locked in. Hold on . . . Pecan? Toucan is what I'm thinking of. It's a root vegetable, isn't it?

Another spectacular *Millionaire* fail came when a contestant was asked, 'What is George W. Bush's first name?' Perhaps she was paranoid it was a trick question because she asked for a 50/50, but then she was confronted with a choice between Edmund and George and STILL somehow managed to pick the wrong answer.

Sometimes, you can understand why someone might be stumped by a seemingly simple question. But, still, what are the odds that 81 per cent of the audience are wrong?

Meredith Viera: Which children's game might start with the phrase 'taking care of business' and end with the phrase 'making carrot biscuits'?

    (a) Hopscotch

    (b) Telephone (aka Chinese whispers)

    (c) Rock, paper, scissors

    (d) Marbles.*

Contestant: Taking care of business . . . taking care of business . . . oh . . . no. [clenched fists in frustration] You know . . . I . . . [decisively] Ask the audience.

Viera: OK, audience. Dana needs your help. Press the buttons to vote now . . . OK. 81 per cent of the audience believe it is: Telephone.

Contestant: Telephone? . . . Telephone? That wasn't what I was thinking.

Meredith: What were you thinking?
Contestant: I was like . . . Hopscotch . . . OK . . . I'm going to have to stop the question [audience groans in frustration].

Meredith: No, no, no [admonishing the audience for its reaction . . .] so let's see if it was Hopscotch or Telephone.

* The answer was Telephone, which provoked more frustrated groans from the audience.

Now, how is your mental arithmetic? Good enough to function under the glare of the lights and cameras? For one *Millionaire* contestant, a nervous giggling wreck of a young woman, the answer was a definite 'no':

Host: What is the minimum number of six-packs you would need to put 99 bottles on the wall [the possible answers were]:

    (a) 15

    (b) 17

    (c) 19

    (d) 21.

Contestant: [laughing] I know . . . It's easy maths but I really can't think right now . . . [manically laughing again] All right, so . . .

Host: OK, take your time. Right, so you have to figure out how many beers in a six-pack . . .
Contestant: How many in a six-pack is six [cue

more laughter]. All right, so six goes into ninety-nine . . . leaves one . . . carry over [now the audience laughs] . . . three . . .

Host: How many six-packs did you drink before you came tonight?
Contestant: [laughing] . . . OK so six times six is forty. No . . . that's eight times something.

Host: Five . . .
Contestant: Five, six . . . so wait, so it would be nineteen then.

Host: . . .
Contestant: [looks to heavens for inspiration, then forwards as though studying an imaginary blackboard] Six, five . . . three . . . [looks at host and puts hands together in prayer] nineteen.

Host: Final answer?
Contestant: Final.

Host: It's not nineteen. It's seventeen. I'm so sorry.

Incidentally, that phrase 'Final answer' means just that. Once uttered, there is no going back. One contestant fell foul of this rule in a spectacular fail:

Meredith Viera: Autosomal Compelling Hello-Opthalmic Outburst syndrome, whose initials offer a clue, is the need to do what when seeing the sun?

(a) Cough

(b) Yawn

(c) Sneeze

(d) Hiccup.

Contestant: Huh . . . Well, you know what Meredith, just by looking at it, I can't say the answer is just jumping out at me.

Viera: Take a minute.
Contestant: Autosomal . . . Compelling . . . Hello . . . Opthalmic . . . Outburst . . .

Viera: [patiently reiterating and emphasizing the wording] . . . whose initials offer a clue, is the need to do what when seeing the sun?
Contestant: Oh, I see now. Achoo. There we go. So let's go (d), final answer [suddenly seeing his mistake and waving hands]. Oh, EXCUSE ME . . . (c)!

Meredith: Oh . . . so sorry, Brian. You said, 'Final answer'. Oh my gosh . . . so sorry.

And while we are gathered here today, let's take a moment to honour the genius of whichever academics used up precious time coming up with the name of

ACHOO syndrome . . . Anyhow, here are some more spectacular *Millionaire* fails:

Host: Denny's Restaurants offer a signature dish named after what sports term,

> (a) Slam Dunk
>
> (b) Touchdown
>
> (c) Knockout
>
> (d) Grand Slam.

Contestant: Slam Dunk, final answer . . . Oops [covers mouth] I meant Grand Slam!

No wonder that schoolteachers often tell students to pay close attention to the question and double check their answers. That's a lesson that this contestant on the Australian version of the show, *Millionaire Hot Seat*, clearly ignored:

Eddie McGuire: Which of these is not a piece of jewellery worn to symbolize a relationship between two people?

> (a) Wedding ring
>
> (b) Engagement ring
>
> (c) Anniversary ring
>
> (d) Burger ring.

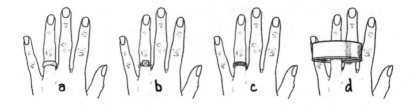

Contestant: Erm, I'm going to go with (b) on that Eddie, anniversary ring, though burger rings are just . . . you know.

Eddie: [kindly] Have another look. Which of these is *not* a piece of jewellery worn to symbolize a relationship between two people?
Contestant: (b) . . . [looks around] What? [the screen illuminates the final answer]
Contestant: [as though explaining it to a simpleton] Relationship, Eddie . . . Wedding and engagement . . .

Eddie: Which . . . is . . . *not* . . . a piece of jewellery. NOT a piece of jewellery.
Contestant: Oh my God, Burger ring! [leans forward] Oh my God, Eddie, that's the most embarrassing thing that has ever happened to me . . . [audience laughs] Oh, my . . . that's so . . . can we just can we just cut and start again?

Eddie: The only thing you got right was when you said that's the most embarrassing thing that would ever happen to you.

If you're worried about the standard of teaching today, one particular UK *Millionaire* episode would have given you food for thought. The contestant was a teacher. He did admit at one point that he had had some problems with his students running out of the classroom, but difficulties with discipline don't always reflect a deficit of knowledge. Or do they?

The third question was, 'Which of the following has a shaft and a barb? (a) Candle, (b) Arrow, (c) Football, (d) Book. His first, confident answer was (d). Host Chris Tarrant was trying hard not to be too obvious in his disbelief, but he did ask a gentle question trying to draw out the logic. The teacher admitted he only had a vague idea of what a shaft was and had never heard of a barb, so the answer (d) had just been a hunch. He conceded that, 'Well, I suppose it *could* be candle. Fortunately, he did at least pick up on the dubious expressions of Chris and the audience and went for a lifeline, which gave the right answer. He then managed to stumble through a few more questions, giving parents around the country a few moments to gather their children and anxiously ask them if he was one of their teachers.

MILLIONAIRE II – FASTEST FINGERS AND CLANGERS

Of course, before the *Millionaire* contestants even start the game, they have to qualify to take the chair by participating in the fastest finger round, in which a group of wannabes try to answer a simple question as fast as possible:

Chris Tarrant: Starting with 'Stop', what is the correct traffic light order, according to the British Highway Code?

> (a) Amber
>
> (b) Red and amber
>
> (c) Red
>
> (d) Green.

Chris Tarrant: If any of our contestants have got that wrong, don't let them give you a lift home. OK then, the right order, we should all know this . . . the right order. Err . . . first, starting with 'stop' is red of course, then comes amber and red, which is sort of get ready, then it's green, which means go, then it's amber which means get ready to stop. That's the right order . . . hopefully all ten got it right but I bet they didn't. So let's see how many got it right . . . [the board stubbornly refuses to light up, showing that no one has got the question right].

Tarrant: Ha, ha ha . . . I love it! I don't believe that . . . right then, we'll try again until we find a question that at least one of you gets right!

Mind you, when it comes to *Millionaire*, even the audience can come up with some clangers. On one occasion, the contestant was forced to resort to the 'Ask the audience' lifeline when confronted with a question about the meaning of the French word *jambon*. Dispiritingly, 11 per cent of the audience plumped for 'jam'.

Now, in defence of the following contestant, this answer came after the US version of the show introduced a fifteen-second limit for the $500 question. She probably still wishes she had gone for Paris Hilton instead:

Meredith Viera: When attacked by a predator, which of these animals will often activate a large gland known as an ink sack?

(a) Cheetah

(b) Squid

(c) Owl

(d) Paris Hilton.

Contestant: Owl, final answer.

Viera: Which of these phrases is a common way of saying I can't take it anymore?

(a) That's the last stick

(b) That's the last leaf

(c) That's the last straw

(d) I'm moving to Canada.

Contestant: (a) That's the last stick, final answer [looks round as audience groans] . . . oh . . . I meant . . .

OK, so it is fair enough if this contestant never saw *The A Team* on TV, but the mind still boggles at this answer:

Viera: 'I pity the fool' is a catchphrase of which famous American?

    (a) Tom Cruise

    (b) Jerry Seinfeld

    (c) Mr T.

    (d) George Washington.

Contestant: George Washington, final answer.

And you have to wonder what kind of flan this contestant had been served:

Question: Which of the following is not made with tortillas?

    (a) Enchilada

    (b) Taco

    (c) Flan

    (d) Burritos.

Contestant: Ermmm . . . Taco?

The first contestant on the US edition of the show to leave with zero prize money was Robby Roseman, who had previously revealed he was wearing his lucky shorts:

Regis Philbin: Hannibal crossed the Alps using what animals?

    Chihuahuas

    rhinoceri

    elephants

    or llamas.

Contestant: [uses the 50:50 to eliminate Chihuahuas and rhinoceri] OK, so . . . llamas? Final answer.

Philbin: You might want to burn those lucky shorts . . .

Ever since, the fans of the show refer to someone who goes out on the first round as a 'llama'.

Another contestant failed the first question, which asked 'After Monday, Tuesday, even the calendar reads . . .? The correct answer, out of four acronyms, was 'WTF' (ie Wednesday, Thursday, Friday). However, the contestant insisted on choosing 'OMG' because 'that's what I say when I realize it's only Wednesday.'

And here's an interesting story from the French version. The question was, '*Qu'est ce qui gravite autour de la Terre?*, i.e. which object rotates around the Earth, with the answer being the Moon, Sun, Mars or Venus. The contestant, who seemed a bit hapless, decided to ask the audience. The surprising thing is that the answers were split between two options, the Moon and the Sun, with about 60 per cent going for the latter.

The contestant foolishly trusted them and was eliminated. There are two possible explanations. One is that the French audience was astronomically challenged. But the second, which has been put forward by a psychologist, is that there is a national tendency for the French to be mischievous and that the audience was intentionally tricking the contestant. *Formidable*!

And now, from the Italian quiz, the question, 'Which of these animals would you see on a perch? (a) Parrot, (b) Hamster, (c) Pig, (d) Turtle.' The immediate problem was that the contestant didn't understand what was meant by a perch. The host suggested she ask the audience, but she steadfastly refused to do so and attempted to logic her way out of the quandary by arguing, 'The perch could be another name to call a hamster wheel . . . and since parrots usually stay on a pirate's shoulder . . . it must be the hamster!'

On the Turkish version of the quiz the host asked, 'On what surfaces are curling, hockey and skate sports? (a) Ice (b) Grass (c) Sand (d) Soil.' The contestant decided to ask the audience, and 91 per cent of them picked (a), with 4 per cent picking (b), 3 per cent (c) and 2 per cent (d). For some reason, he was still undecided so chose to go 50:50. This eliminated (b) and (c), leaving him with a straight choice of ice or trusting the 2 per cent of the audience who had chosen soil. Incredibly, he went with soil.

And finally, another classic from the Italian version. I heard this story from an American man who had moved to Italy to live with his Italian wife, and ended up watching an episode of *Who Wants to Be a Millionaire?* with her family. His Italian was less than perfect, so he reported the whole experience as being like watching an extremely dramatic opera that he only partly understood, so let's picture it that way. The show, *Chi vuol essere milionario?*, starts with a limited number of options for the easy questions. In this case the contestant, an innocent-looking young man who would be playing the tragically doomed hero, was faced with only two options for the answer to what is the colour of the Ferrari Formula 1 team: red or yellow. He answered . . . yellow.

At this point the drama moved up a notch. The

Italian wife and her family were immediately on their feet muttering half-understood Italian curses at the TV. The camera closed in on the master of ceremonies, who was visibly stunned, then panned across the chorus – the audience – who were in various poses of shock and anger. (For Italians, F1 is a religion and Ferrari are its high priests. Not knowing its colour is red is like not knowing that Man Utd play in red or thinking the US president lives in the Yellow House.)

The quizmaster offered the tragic hero a chance to avert his fate. As if the shock on the faces of the audience wasn't enough, the camera picked out the contestant's wife, with a face of thunder, and his children, watching their hero crumble in front of them.

In spite of the warning, our hero insisted on embracing his doom and told the host to lock in the answer of yellow. He had the dreadful over-confidence, or hubris, that is the downfall of many a tragic hero. Perhaps he was thinking of Ferrari's corporate logo, which is indeed yellow, but it was clear there would be no redemption for this sinner. Cue howls of anger from the TV-watching family, pandemonium in the studio audience and a close up of his wife's face as she plotted divorce, murder and worse. All that was missing was a Wagnerian trumpet ushering in the demons of hell.

The host, shaking with repressed emotion, informed the contestant of his error. At this moment in the opera, the stage would have been plunged into darkness with a single spotlight picking out our hero as he realized his catastrophic pact with the devil.

He was alone on-stage, knowing his future had just turned to dust.

As Bill Shankly (the old Liverpool manager) didn't say, game shows are NOT a matter of life and death. They are much more than that!

QUICKFIRE ROUND III

See if you can come up with better, or even funnier, answers

Q: Cognac is a fine brandy made from the juice of which fruit?
A: Coconut.

Q: In the *Beano* comic, which character is known as 'the Minx'?
A: Dodger.

Q: What is the highest double-digit number?
A: 25.

Q: Traditionally, what liquid is said to be poured on troubled waters?
A: Cold water.

Q: Which letter in the word 'colour' is not used in
the American spelling?
A: O.

Q: What's 14 + 16?
A: 20.

Q: Elderly people are described as being what
'. . . in the tooth'?
A: Old.

Q: A person who is eccentric is often described as
having what animals '. . . in the belfry'?
A: Pigs.

Q: What is 360 ÷ 3?
A: 360.

Q: An annual event takes place how many times a
year?
A: Twelve.

Q: The bushwhacker and outlaw Ned Kelly was born in which country?
A: Canada.

Q: What is the three-letter name of the area which is the background for the Sun, Moon and stars?
A: Sea.

Q: At the seaside, novelty shops sell hats with the slogan, what '. . . me quick'?
A: Whip.

Q: Which surname is shared by a real cowboy called Butch and a fictional one called Hopalong?
A: Lesbian.

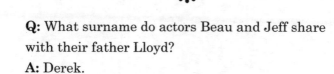

Q: What surname do actors Beau and Jeff share with their father Lloyd?
A: Derek.

Q: The (UK) National Space Centre is based in which Midlands city?
A: Chicago.

Q: What is 23 + 28?
A: 48.

Q: In law, the principle that a person cannot be tried twice for the same offence is called 'Double . . .' what?
A: Whammy.

WHAT WOULD WILL
HAVE SAID?

Of course, quiz show fails are often a collision between the personal tragedy of public embarrassment
and the outright comedic, which can be enjoyed by
pretty much everyone except the hapless contestant
and possibly their humiliated partners. But how do
our contestants succeed when it comes to answering
questions on the arts, from Hamlet to *King Kong*?
(We'll come to music in the next section.) Well, naturally, since we are taking a biased approach in which
we only include the stupidest answers, it turns out
that they do pretty badly, starting with the one and
only:

From *The Weakest Link* (BBC)

Anne Robinson: Iago and Desdemona are
characters in which Shakespeare play?
Contestant: I did English literature at university.
Um . . . *Hamlet?*

Robinson: The action of which Shakespeare play takes place between dusk on January 5th and dawn on January 6th?
Contestant: *A Midsummer Night's Dream.*

From *This Morning* (ITV)

Richard Madeley: Who wrote *Othello*?
Contestant: . . . No idea.

Madeley: He also wrote *Hamlet*.
Contestant: Pass.

From *Family Fortunes* (BBC)

Host: A Shakespeare play with a name in it.
Contestant: *A Midsummers' Night Dream* . . .

Host: You mean *A Midsummer Night's Dream* . . .
Contestant: [nods, then with the host goes to the answer board but it comes up blank]

Host: Hang on, where's the name in that?
Contestant: Summer's a name . . . There's lots of little girls called Summer.

Host: [clearly stumped]

From *Pointless* (BBC), in a round on Famous Williams

Alexander Armstrong: Who wrote *Hamlet*?
Contestant: William . . .

Armstrong: [raises eyebrows in expectation of a correct answer]
Contestant: . . . Tell?

And now to everything from myths to *The Wizard of Oz:*

From *The Weakest Link* (BBC)

Anne Robinson: In which European country was actor Antonio Banderas born?
Contestant: Mexico.

Robinson: In ancient mythology, how many labours did Hercules do?
Contestant: One.

Robinson: Which movie ended with the famous words, 'It was beauty that killed the beast'?*
Answer: Pass.

* The first, 1933 *King Kong*, often misquoted as 'Twas beauty killed the beast'.

Robinson: The nineteenth-century novel by the Russian author Dostoevsky is *Crime and . . .* what?

Contestant: [decisively] *Prejudice.*

Robinson: Which Emily Brontë novel features the characters Catherine Earnshaw and Heathcliff?

Contestant: *Treasure Island.*

Robinson: What body part did the Tin Man ask Dorothy to get him?

Answer: A brain.

Robinson: Sancho Panza was the companion of which famous fictional character?

Contestant: Rupert Bear.

From *Pointless* (BBC)

Alexander Armstrong: Who wrote the novels *Persuasion* and *Northanger Abbey*?

[David and Sarah are competing as a team: it's David's turn to answer]
David: [confidently] Jane Eyre!
Sarah: [immediately cringes, then laughs]

From Rock FM Radio

Host: Name a film starring Bob Hoskins that is also the name of a famous painting by Leonardo Da Vinci.
Contestant: *Who Framed Roger Rabbit?*

Host: Complete the title of this novel by Henry James: *The Turn of the* . . .
Contestant: Century.

Host: Complete the title of the well-known play, *The Iceman* . . .
Contestant: Melts.

Host: In literature, poet Philip Larkin was born in what century?
A: The seventeenth.

Host: In Tolkien's *Lord of the Rings* trilogy, the third and final book is called *The Return of the* . . . what?
Contestant: *Jedi.*

From *Dog Eat Dog* (BBC)

Ulrika Jonsson: Who wrote *Lord of the Rings*?
Contestant: Enid Blyton.

From *The French Quiz* (LBC Radio)

Host: Which French author has been translated into more languages than any other French author in the world?
Contestant: Chaucer.

From *The National Lottery Show* (BBC)

Host: What's the name of the playwright commonly known by the initials G.B.S.?
Contestant: William Shakespeare?

From *This Morning* (ITV)

Host: On which street did Sherlock Holmes live?
Contestant: . . .

Host: He makes bread?
Contestant: Err . . .

Host: He makes cakes . . .
Contestant: Kipling Street?

From *National Lottery Jet Set* (BBC)

Host: What year is the title of a famous novel by George Orwell?
Contestant: 1949.

From *The* Danny Kelly Show
(BBC Radio WM)

Danny Kelly: Which French Mediterranean town hosts a famous film festival every year?
Contestant: I don't know . . . I need a clue.

Kelly: OK. What do beans come in?
Contestant: . . . Cartons?

And finally, the face of the wonderful, quick-witted host Graeme Garden (once of The Goodies) was a picture after this exchange on *Beat The Nation* (Channel 4):

Graeme Garden: The Ashmolean in Oxford was England's first what?
Contestant: Indian restaurant.

AND AS FOR MUSIC...

I'm trying to be fair to the contestants throughout this book: we can all watch reels of bloopers on the internet, or read lists of idiotic quiz show answers and feel smug that we are not as dumb as the hapless participants, but deep down we also all know that 'There but for the grace of God go I'. The pressure of the situation must be intense, and this obviously produces some strange psychological effects. In addition, there are subjects such as music where everyone has a partial knowledge. You may be an expert in chamber music of the eighteenth century, but utterly clueless about pop music after 1960. By contrast, you can have a deep knowledge of late twentieth century easy listening, but know nothing whatsoever about opera. So let's bear that in mind when we look at these hopeless music answers.

The joy here often lies in how incongruous the answers are. For instance, this contestant from BBC's *Pointless* couldn't be more confused:

Alexander Armstrong: We need a top ten UK hit by Madonna.

Contestant: I'll take a guess and say 'Knees Up Mother Brown'.

Then we get lowbrow answers to highbrow questions:

From *The Weakest Link* (BBC)

Anne Robinson: The *Hallelujah Chorus* appears in which oratorio by Handel?

Contestant: The *Sound of Music*?

And highbrow answers to lowbrow questions:

From *Steve Wright in the Afternoon* (BBC Radio)

Steve Wright: Who wrote the music for 'Moon River' and 'The Pink Panther'?

Contestant: . . . Mendelssohn.

But more often than not, we find contestants who are simply wrong, wrong, wrong:

In *321* (ITV), a creaking UK game show, one round involved the contestant trying to find an answer that had already been heavily hinted at *in the question*. You really do feel for the host:

Ted Rogers: This is a composer. German by birth, English by adoption. Best known for an oratorio published in 1741. It was called *Messiah*. You're bound to know his handle.

Female contestant: [pressing buzzer] Oh God, I used to have it at school . . . Handel's *Water Music*.

Rogers: So, who's the composer?

Female Contestant: Chopin? [audience laughter as Rogers gives her a disbelieving look]

Rogers: [shrugs and turns to next contestant] So I can offer it to you . . .

Male Contestant: Beethoven?

Rogers: [looks at audience in a parody of despair as the laughter intensifies]

Host: In what century was the composer J.S. Bach born?

Contestant: The twentieth century.

From *The Weakest Link* (BBC)

Anne Robinson: In 1987, the Bangles had a number one UK hit with the song 'Walk Like an . . . '?

Contestant one: Stranger.

Contestant two: Gandhi?

Robinson: What nationality was the composer Sir Edward Elgar?
Contestant: Norwegian.

Robinson: In music, what was the first name of the German composer Bach, who was born in 1685?
Contestant: Edward?

From *The Ken Bruce Show* (BBC Radio)

Ken Bruce: Listen to this piece of music [cue 'Sex Crime' by the Eurythmics] then tell me the name of the movie it featured in, based on a famous George Orwell novel.
Contestant: Was it 1989?

Host: Name a famous rock band that starts with the word 'The'.
Contestant: The Kiss.

From *24 Hour Quiz* (ITV)

Host: Who sang the song '*Je t'aime, moi non plus*' with Jane Birkin?
Contestant: Jacques Chirac

From *Notts and Crosses* (BBC Radio Nottingham)

Jeff Owen: Which classical composer became deaf in later life: Ludwig van ... ?

Contestant: [with complete confidence] Van Gogh.

From *The National Lottery Show* (BBC)

Eamonn Holmes: Dizzy Gillespie is famous for playing ... what?

Contestant: [looks up and then down] Basketball?

Then there was the caller to Radio Norfolk whom the presenter tried to help answer the question, 'Who had a worldwide hit with "What a Wonderful World".' The painful series of hints spelt out the name, syllable by syllable:

Host: What do you call the part between your hand and your elbow?
Contestant: . . . Arm.

Host: That's correct. And if you're not weak, you are . . . ?
Contestant: . . . Strong.

Host: Yes. And what was Lord Mountbatten's first name?
Contestant: . . . Louis.

Host: Well, there we go then. So . . . who had a worldwide hit with 'What a Wonderful World'?
Contestant: . . . Frank Sinatra.

EARLY MORNING BLUES

This Morning (ITV) is a UK morning magazine show that has become something of a national institution. At its best, regular hosts Philip Schofield and Holly Willoughby, backed up by Ruth and Eamonn Holmes, steer an effortless path from frivolous fashion to heart-wrenching accounts of abuse, and from cookery and the Kardashians to current affairs. During the coronavirus lockdown the show was unexpectedly given the status of being an 'essential service', and remained on-air with social distancing in place and most guests appearing via videolink. The result was an increasingly shambolic, comical show in which Phil and Holly's tendency to dissolve into giggles was exacerbated by regular, amateurish moments where the skeleton crew struggled to cope.

During this period the show featured the regular giveaway quiz, spin to win. A wheel, cheaply constructed from wood, nails and glitter, would descend from the ceiling; viewers could win a spin simply by phoning in and remembering the password of the day from the show's website. On at least one occasion, a wheel malfunction led to Holly hastily scribbling the prize amounts on torn up bits of her script so they could pick them out of a bowl left over from the cookery slot.

After the pointer settled on a prize ranging from £500 to £3000, the contestant was offered a supplementary question, generally of insulting simplicity, based on the immediately preceding items on the show. The additional prize, which also descended from the ceiling, was a bag of what Phil referred to as 'shizzle': branded cups and T-shirts, leftover cosmetics from the day's show and, usually, a jigsaw with a picture of Phil and Holly. On this occasion the jigsaw had a picture of them in a notorious episode in which they turned up tipsy after an all-nighter at the National Television Awards, and then presented part of the show while sprawled out on the sofa in their gladrags.

The correct answer to the question below was 'Prince Philip', the ageing husband of the ageing queen. As luck would have it, another national treasure, the grande dame actress Judi Dench, was waiting via videolink for her interview, and Phil and Holly spent the preamble to the segment imploring contestants not to 'let Dame Judi down'. And what happened?

Philip: So, to win the shizzle, all you have to do is answer the question.

Holly: And the question is . . . Which member of the royal family turned ninety-nine today?

Caller: Oh my god, I can't even think of his name . . . [pauses, then calls to someone at her end of the phone] Max! [no response]

Philip: [pointing at himself to avoid confusion] What's my name?

Caller: uh . . . Philip.

Philip: AND HE WOULD BE . . . ?

Caller: He's ninety-nine!

Philip: [patiently gesturing in encouragement] And his name is . . .

Caller: I'm too nervous, I've gone blank . . .

Philip: No, no, no, what's my name?

Caller: Philip.

Philip: [getting desperate] What's his name?

Caller: . . . King Philip?

Philip: [seamlessly] Absolutely, well done . . .

On another recent occasion the answer to the question was easy – the Duchess of Cambridge, the former Kate Middleton, Britain's next queen, to whom Phil and Holly had just been speaking on air. But the caller needed some prompting, so Holly intervened:

Holly: OK, just tell me who it was we were just talking to . . .
Caller: [agonized pause] Princess Diana?

Now for another demonstration of the perils of giving contestants hints, and the many ways it can go kaput. Phil and Holly had been talking to Len Goodman, ex-judge on the BBC dancing competition *Strictly Come Dancing* about the lettuces he had been growing during the coronavirus lockdown. They had also conducted a longish interview with an internet vacuum cleaner guru (I promise you, I'm not making this up), which was why they had a nifty hand-held cleaner to give away. And nothing was going to stop them:

Holly: Now, to win this, you just have to answer the question . . . which *Strictly* judge were we just talking to?
Contestant: Errrm . . .

Holly: He's not there anymore . . .
Contestant: . . .

Phil: Do you watch *Strictly*?
Contestant: I saw him. But I can't remember his name . . .

Holly: It rhymes with 'pen' . . . and it starts with a 'luh' . . .

Contestant: Errr . . . I mean . . .

Phil: It rhymes with 'pen' but it doesn't have a 'P', it has an 'L' . . .
Contestant: . . .

Phil: [impatiently] Try 'Len' . . .
Contestant: . . .

Holly: JUST SAY 'LEN'!!!!
Contestant: . . . Len.

Phil and Holly: Yessss [they give her the prize and say goodbye].
Phil: Some people just won't be helped.

And if you thought that was bad:

Phil: [giving hints to a confused caller] It's an Australian animal . . .
Holly: Small Australian animal.
Phil: Lives in a tree . . .
Both: [mime a koala, pretending their fingers are claws]
Caller: [extended silence]
Phil: [responding to producer's voice in his ear] What?? She's gone! [turns to Holly] We've managed to find every single way this game could go wrong.

Which brings us to Richard and Judy. Phil and Holly inherited their role in the national institution that is *This Morning* from Richard Madeley and Judy Finnegan, who hosted the show from 1988 to 2001. If you aren't familiar with them, imagine Richard as a handsome Labrador, with a horribly dated haircut that comes dangerously close to being a mullet: always enthusiastic and totally confident, even when he is spouting nonsense, while his slightly older, far more sensible wife Judy is the sharp, self-possessed journalist who barely suppresses her impatience at his many *faux pas* when he's right next to her. I once heard Richard memorably summed up as being the sort of man who, if you say you've been to Tenerife, will tell you he's been to Elevenerife.

Anyhow, they hosted many quizzes, often designed to be easy giveaways to viewers. In spite of this, the quizzes were a rich seam of stupidity, like these three callers who wouldn't take a hint:

> **Judy:** The American television show *The Sopranos* is about opera – true or false?
> **Contestant:** Er . . . true.

> **Judy:** No, actually, it's about the mafia. But it is an American TV show, so I'll give you that . . .

Richard: In which US state would you find Los Angeles, San Francisco and lots of big bears?
Contestant: Florida.

Richard: No . . . it's on the other side.
Contestant: . . .

Judy: [awkwardly singing] 'I wish they all could be da da da da girls . . .'
Contestant: New York?

Richard: Who was Bill Clinton's vice-president?
Contestant: I don't know.

Richard: [patronizingly] Come on . . . he also stood for president himself. You know, Al . . .
Contestant: Al Jolson.

And now for some more Q's and A's:

Q: Which Danish city is famous for its statue of a mermaid?
A: Denmark.

Q: What is origami?
A: A herb.

Q: Which Spanish island is famous for hosting lots of trendy parties?
A: Spain.

Q: How many metres are there in a kilometre?
A: Three.

Q: Which American actor is married to Nicole Kidman?
A: Forrest Gump.

Q: At what time is *Midday Money* broadcast?
A: 12.15?

Q: On what date does New Year's Day fall?
A: The thirty-first.

Q: When was the battle of Hastings?
A: 1866.

Q: How many minutes are there in three quarters of an hour?
A: Sixty.

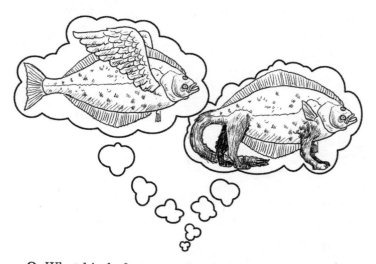

Q: What kind of creature is a halibut?
A: A bird.

Q: No, wrong. Try again.
A: A ferret.

Q: What gifts did the Three Wise Men bring to the Baby Jesus?
A: Gold, platinum and silver.

Q: Which country was ruled by Tsars . . . France or Russia?
A: France.

Q: If you spoke Dutch, what country would you be from?
A: Denmark.

Q: In which direction do the hands of a clock travel?
A: Anti-clockwise.

Q: If I travel at 60 miles an hour, how far do I travel in ten minutes?
A: 20,000 miles.

One of the high or low points, depending on your point of view, of the Richard and Judy experience, was the game *You Say, We Play*. Pictures of everyday objects or celebrities were projected on a screen behind the pair: contestants had to describe the subject of the image, and give hints so that Richard and Judy could give the correct answer to win money. Some of Richard's guesses in particular could be pricelessly stupid:

Contestant: You step in it and it takes you up and down to different floors.
Richard: . . . Dog poo?

MORE INNUENDO: *FAMILY FEUD* AND *COUNTDOWN*

Family Feud (CBS) is an endless source of bizarre answers that reveal the slightly dubious workings of the human mind. Here are a few more examples of contestants being goaded into rude or inappropriate answers by the twisted question masters of the show.

Steve Harvey: Name something that gets up in the morning before you do.
Female Contestant: Sorry, Mom, but for men, their penis.
Male contestant (husband of the above): [speechless with laughter]

Harvey: Good answer, good answer . . . [shakes his head in mock disapproval at husband, who is still speechless].

Louie Anderson: Name something teenage boys can do for hours at a time.
Contestant: Masturbate.

Anderson: Name a part of the body that gets bigger as adults get older.
Contestant: Uh . . . penis.

Steve Harvey: Name something that doesn't fall apart while you're on it.
Elderly male contestant: My wife . . .

Harvey: Tell me a part of the body that starts with the letter 'T'.
Young male contestant: Titties . . . [applauds himself when audience starts to laugh].

Harvey: Name something you practised kissing when you were a kid.
Male contestant: [slightly shamefaced] Sister . . .

Harvey: When people talk about 'the big one', what do they refer to?
Female contestant: A man's privates?

Host: Name a phrase some husbands dread hearing.
Female contestant (beside her husband): 'Honey, I'm home . . .' [pulls abashed face at her own suggestion].

Harvey: Name a job that's dirty but someone had to do it.
Contestant: Plumber [buzzer indicates this answer has already been given] . . . gynaecologist?

Harvey: What might a male dog give to a female dog?
Contestant (a buttoned-down young man): Well . . . I don't know how to phrase this, but . . . himself.

Harvey: [says nothing but turns to contestant with an eyebrow raised]
Contestant: Make love . . . doggy love?

Harvey: . . .
Contestant: [in desperation] Doggy style?

Harvey: Name something your doctor does to you that he doesn't enjoy any more than you do.
Contestant: Sticking his hand up your butt.

Harvey: Name something that doctors routinely pull out of patients?
Contestant: Hamsters?

Harvey: What does your husband do when he runs out of clean underwear?
Wife: He wears a pair of mine . . . [laughs].
Husband: [says nothing, but makes hand-across-throat DON'T GO THERE gesture]
Wife: [screams and laughs louder]

Harvey: Name something Judge Judy might be wearing under her robe.

Male contestant: [indicates his chest, at nipple height] A garter . . . an . . . undergarment.

Harvey: What you doing this for? [pulls his jacket out to two peaks] What have you got to say about Judge Judy?

In the popular UK quiz show *Countdown* (Channel 4), the co-presenter picks out letters from a rack, then contestants have thirty seconds to make the longest word they can. Obviously, some of the funniest moments have come when the letters are in danger of spelling out something . . . well . . . the unexpected. Try this:

W . . . J . . . K . . . A . . . E . . . A . . . Y . . . R . . .

At which point the co-presenter Rachel Riley picked out an 'N' and gave a slightly awkward smile saying, 'Oh . . . good . . .' One contestant managed to resist the obvious and went for the six-letter word 'Awaken', but the other could only manage 'Wanker'.

On another occasion Riley's predecessor, Carol Vorderman, allowed herself a short laugh as the first four letters were 'C . . . U . . . N . . . T . . .', then became increasingly awkward as the remainder of the letters continued giving:

'C . . . U . . . N . . . T . . . F . . . L . . . A . . . P . . . S'.

Richard Whiteley, the main presenter, asked the contestants for their answers:

Contestant 1: I'll go with the board . . .

And now, from the same quiz:

Contestant: I'll have a vowel please.

Carol Vorderman: [pulling letters from a rack and calling them out] 'O'.

Contestant: I'll have a consonant.

Vorderman: 'R'.

Contestant: I'll have a consonant.

Vorderman: 'G'.

Contestant: And a vowel please.

Vorderman: 'A' [freezes for a second and puts her head briefly in her hand].

Contestant: I'll have a consonant.

Vorderman: [after a momentary pause] I don't know if it's worse, but that's an 'N'.

* * *

SPEAKING OF INNUENDO

As we've mentioned, the American equivalent (and predecessor) of *Mr and Mrs* (ITV) is *The Newlywed Game* (ABC). This exchange involved an attractive blonde bride who unfortunately, egged on by the host, went a long way to single-handedly reinforcing prejudices about blondes. Although given a slightly knowing look in her eye, it's possible she knew exactly what she was doing and was putting on a parody:

Host: Would you say your husband is more rural or urban?
Guest: Heck, I don't know what they mean.
Host: You'd know . . . you married him. So which is he?
Guest: [shrugs] Urban, I guess.
Host: And how long has he been that way.
Guest: About two months . . .
Host: And is there anything he can do about it?
Guest: He went to a doctor . . .
Host: And did he give him anything for his urban?
Guest: He gave *me* something . . . [extended laughter]

* * *

THE THREE 'R'S – READING, RITING AND RITHMETIC

The term dates back to at least the early nineteenth century and may be rooted in earlier references to reading, recitation and reckoning. It has mainly been used over the years to urge some kind of 'back to basics' approach to education, often to support the argument that modern youth are lacking in these key skills and that it is the fault of the parents, the teachers or some other handy scapegoat. The fact that every generation believes that the next one is woefully undereducated suggests that this may be a prejudice that hits us as we age. In fact the evidence from quiz shows suggests that basic failures of spelling, comprehension and numeracy are pretty equally spread across all ages: the basic errors below come from contestants from pretty much every age range, and a wide range of quiz shows and game shows.

Host: How many 'e's are there in 'argument'?
Contestant: [pause] . . . Three.

From *Steve Wright in the Afternoon* (BBC Radio)

Steve Wright: How many days are there in five weeks?
Contestant: . . . I don't know.

Wright: Well, give it a guess.
Contestant: 60?

And what can you do with a caller who won't even take the most blindingly obvious hint? This is from the Bob Hope Birthday Quiz:

Host: Bob Hope was the fifth of how many sons?
Contestant: Four?

Or even worse, from *Family Feud* (CBS):

Richard Karn: How much does an ounce of gold weigh?
Contestant: 14 ounces.

Phil Wood: What's eleven squared?
Contestant: I don't know.

Wood: I'll give you a clue. It's two ones with a two in the middle.
Contestant: Is it five?

From *The Paul Wappat Show*
(BBC Radio Newcastle)

Paul Wappat: How long did the Six-Day War between Egypt and Israel last?

Contestant: [excruciating pause] . . . Fourteen days?

From *The Weakest Link* (BBC)

Anne Robinson: Which hot drink is 'eat' an anagram of?

Contestant: Hot chocolate?

Robinson: What 'G' is a brand of animal-shaped cheddar crackers introduced by Pepperidge Farm in 1962?

Contestant: Oreos.

Robinson: How many 'I's are there in 'intelligent'?

Contestant: One.

Robinson: What does the 'U' stand for in the name of the dissolved country USSR?

Contestant: Russia.

Robinson: In traffic, what 'J' is where two roads meet?

Contestant: Dual carriageway.

[The only puzzle is why this contestant thought that two-lane roads were named jewel motorways.]

Robinson: The equator divides the world into how many hemispheres?

Contestant: Three.

Robinson: In maths, what is one half as a decimal?

Contestant: A quarter.

Robinson: In sport, the name of which famous racehorse is the word 'murder' spelt backwards?

Contestant: . . . Shergar?

Robinson: Introduced in Britain in 1978, the State Earnings Related Pension Scheme is better known by what acronym?

Contestant: PAYE.

Robinson: Which three-letter word is known as the definite article?
Contestant: . . . 'It'?

From *Blockbusters* (ITV)

Host: What 'U' are the Eastern Europeans who originated the tradition of painting on Easter eggs?
Contestant: Yugoslavians.

Host: What kind of dozen is thirteen?
Contestant: Half a dozen.

Host: In medicine, what word beginning with 'g' represents the area of medicine specializing in the treatment of the elderly?
Contestant: Gynaecology.

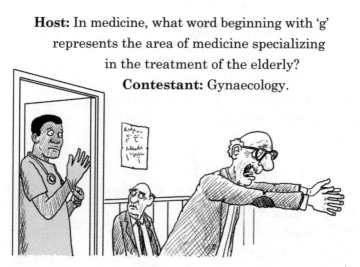

Of course, people often blame the teachers for the state of our children's education. And unfortunately, a teacher occasionally puts their head over the parapet of a game show and suggests this might be true. So here is Shaun, a teacher from Manchester, appearing on *Pointless* (BBC):

Alexander Armstrong: We gave 100 people eleven seconds to name as many US states with a coastline as they could . . . Shaun, how good is your US geography?

Shaun: Now, my geography altogether isn't good. It's my weakest subject . . . I can hear a lot of pupils thinking, 'Oh my God, I can't believe you don't know this . . .' so I'm just gonna go for anything and I'm gonna say . . . Mexico?

Armstrong: [stunned] You're going to say Mexico? So . . . let's see how many people said, 'Mexico' [the answer board indicates that this is an incorrect answer]. There are a lot of pupils in Manchester screaming things at the television now, Shaun . . . Richard?

Richard Osman (adjudicator): Mexico? Well . . . it's hard to know where to start here. I think the first thing I'm going to do is write a letter to the education authority of . . . [audience laughter] Mexico . . . it's uh . . . it's not a US state! It's a country!

From *15 to 1* (Channel 4)

Host: From the NATO phonetic alphabet, Papa, Quebec, Romeo, what comes next?
Contestant: Delta.

Now, maths can scare people at the best of times, and when you're under searing television lights it does not help. But still, as these examples from *The Weakest Link* (BBC) prove, if you're going to take a wild guess at an answer, at least make sure it isn't blindingly, obviously wrong:

Q: What is the highest prime number under ten?
A: Eleven.

Q: What is the only even prime number?
A: Nine.

Taking innumeracy one step further, here is one contestant's response to the prompting of host Phil Tufnell on ITV's short-lived quiz show *Simply the Best*:

Phil Tufnell: How many Olympic games have been held?
Contestant: Six.

Tufnell: [gesticulating over enthusiastically]
Higher!!!
Contestant: . . . Five?

Meanwhile, I suspect this answer from Radio 1's early morning show is down to a combination of brain freeze and 'Echo Syndrome', whereby the contestant simply joins together sounds from the question to form something that sounds like an answer, but isn't:

Host: How many toes would three people have in total?
Contestant: Twenty-three.

The only alternative suggestion I can come up with, given that twenty-three isn't even divisible by three, is that this particular contestant came from a family of hobbit-like creatures who really did have varying numbers of toes. Sometimes the most unlikely explanation is the truth!

QUICKFIRE ROUND IV

See if you can come up with better, or even funnier, answers

Q: What 'L' is the name given to the poet who wins the Nobel prize?
A: Leaf.

Q: A type of airship is named after Ferdinand von . . . who?
A: Trapp.

Q: In the film *Deliverance*, a scene involves a duo between stringed instruments: a guitar and a what?
A: Cello.

Q: When people watch too much TV they are warned that which part of their body will turn square?
A: Backside.

Q: Who was prime minister when England won the Soccer World Cup in 1966?
A: Woodrow Wilson.

Q: When someone makes a century in cricket how many runs do they score?
A: Two.

Q: What is the three-letter word for the outside edge of a wheel?
A: Hubcap.

Q: The American swimmer who wrote a book called *The Million Dollar Mermaid* was called Esther what?
A: Rantzen.

Q: The towns of El Paso and San Antonio are in which US state?
A: South America.

Q: Which member of the royal family appeared on *A Question of Sport* in 1979?
A: Ricky Tomlinson.

Q: Apart from Earth, which planet in our solar system begins with a vowel?
A: Pluto.

Q: The word 'knowledgeable' begins with which letter?
A: . . . N?

Hereward
the Wake

Hereward
the Horrible

Q: The Anglo-Saxon king who deposed William the Conqueror was 'Hereward the . . .' what?
A: Horrible.

Q: What is two thirds of 69?
A: 30.

Q: The Groucho Marx film is called *Animal . . .* what?
A: *Instincts*.

Q: Which city was the capital of New Zealand until it was replaced by Wellington?
A: New Guinea.

Q: The poem by Rudyard Kipling is called 'Gunga . . .' what?
A: Ho.

Q: What is the cube root of a thousand?
A: A million.

WHEEL OF MORON

We've seen numerous examples of bloopers from the US show *Wheel of Fortune* (CBS). The show runs five days a week, so it isn't surprising that there are many idiotic moments to choose from, but it's nonetheless a bit startling to see how many different ways contestant can find to avoid getting the correct answer. Here's a round-up of just a small proportion of them. First, note that you can fail the quiz if you fill in the board of letters completely but still find yourself unable to say the word or phrase correctly:

With the board reading **PRISTINELY.**
Contestant: Prist-a-nell-y??

The board read **OVERHAND SQUARE & SHEEPSHANK ARE TYPES. . .**
Contestant: Overhand . . . square and . . . sheep's hank are types . . . ?

The boards read **FLAMENCO DANCE LESSONS.**

Contestant: Flamingo Dance Lessons . . .

At one point the Megaword section of the show required the US host, Pat Sajak, to award the points only if the contestant could correctly use the 8–13 letter word on the board correctly. One contestant's attempt at doing this was: 'Being on Wheel of Fortune is a BOMBASTIC experience!' Sajak hated overseeing this round and would often let the most absurd of sentences pass as 'correct'.

The board read **K _ L L   T H E   _ M P _ R E**

Contestant: Kill the vampire.

The board read **A _ R A H A M   _ I N C O _ N**

Contestant: Abraham Bincoln.

Sajak: I guess Bincoln would be the guy who delivered the Bettysburg address [although Sajak admitted years later that making the joke probably didn't help the poor contestant].

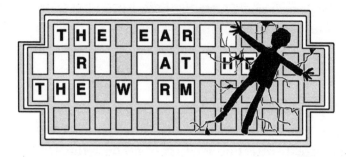

The board read **T H E   E A R _ _   _ _ R _**
_ A T _ H E S   T H E   W _ R M

Contestant: The earth bird catches the worm.

The board read **R E G I S T E R E D   _ _ T E R**

Contestant 1: 'L' [she gets another spin], 'A'.

Sajak: No . . .

Contestant 1: Oh, I didn't know that . . .

Contestant 2: 'W'.

Contestant 3: 'M'.

Sajak: Maybe I should call a letter . . .

[Next there is a speed round, and the contestants continue to guess the wrong letters, going for 'P', 'K', 'B' and 'N'. They do finally stumble on 'V' and then 'O', apparently more by accident than design.]

The board read _ A N C _ T _ A T
Contestant: [guessing the second word] Twat?

The board read _ _ T H _ _ S T _ _ _ N H _ S _ _ N
_ _ _ _ _

Contestant 1: Put her stuff in his darn thing?

Sajak: Oh, so close . . .
Contestant 2: Put hot stew in his own?
Contestant 3: Let him stew on his own money . . .?

Sajak: . . . I'll help: the correct answer is 'Let him stew in his own juice'.

The board read _ I N _ E R S & _ O E S
Contestant: Miners & hoes? [audience laughter]

Sajak: We're laughing with you . . .

The board read A N _ _ _ Y C H I L D
Contestant: An ugly child?

Sajak: Now, you *are* a school counsellor.

And this is from the Australian version:

The board read: _ _ _ **I R E   _ I C K E T**
B A T S M A N
Contestant: Umpire Cricket Batsman?

[Things get worse as the audience applauds, collectively assuming he is right, and the assistant Sophie goes to uncover the remaining letters before being stopped by the host Rob who has to explain the answer is incorrect. The correct answer is UMPIRE WICKET BATSMAN.]

The next series of gaffes are remarkable not only for their vacuity, but also for the eventual outcome:

The board read **F _ Z Z _ _   B _ _ R***
Contestant 1: Fuzzie Bear.
Contestant 2: [calls for an 'E' meaning the board read **F _ Z Z _ _ B E _ R**]
Fizzy Bear . . . Fuzzy Bear . . . Fonzie Bear.

* The correct answer is 'Fozzie Bear'.

The board read **T_ _ S E _ R E T**
Contestant 1: The Secret.
Contestant 2: Too Secret [then the host gives the answer of Top Secret].
Contestant 2: Oh, that was so easy!

The board read **K N _ C K L _ _ _ _D*** and the category is Person
Contestant 1: Nickelodeon?

* It then takes the other four more incorrect guesses at the remaining letters before they come to KNUCKLEHEAD as the correct answer.

The board read
_O _O _O AN_ A _OTTLE OF RUM
Contestant 1: Yo Yo Yo and a bottle of rum.
Contestant 2: Ho Ho Ho and a bottle of rum?

The board read
A _ _ _LAND NEW ZEALAND
Contestant 1: Avaland?

Contestant 2: Archland.
Contestant 3: [chooses a 'K' so the board reads:

A _ _ K L A N D   N E W   Z E A L A N D]
Contestant 3: Ackland?
Contestant 1: [chooses a 'U', giving . . .
A U _ K L A N D   N E W   Z E A L A N D]
Contestant 1: [sounding incredibly doubtful]
Auckland?

Sajak: Correct!
Contestant 1: . . . Well, I've never heard of it.

Sajak: Well, it is the capital of New Zealand.*

* OK pedants, this is actually incorrect since
Wellington is the capital, but hey, you don't watch
game shows to learn stuff.

A BRIEF HISTORY OF THE WORLD

Maybe it's just me, and perhaps I've been watching too many quiz shows and blooper reels, but I like to imagine a future world in which academics are having to piece together the history of the world just by watching our contestants' appearances. What nonsensical conclusions might they come to? And why is it that so many quiz contestants have such a woeful grasp of history? One possible reason is suggested by this delightfully frank answer to this question:

From *Steve Wright in the Afternoon*
(BBC Radio)

Steve Wright: In 1863, which American president gave the Gettysburg Address?
Contestant: I don't know . . . it was before I was born.

This contestant on *The Weakest Link* makes the same point, but even more eloquently:

Anne Robinson: In prisoner of war camps during World War Two, what 'T' was the kind of underground passage that was frequently dug as a means of escape?
Contestant: Herbal tea?

Robinson: [rolling her eyes] Nearly . . . It was 'tunnel'.

[the sharp-tongued host smartly returned to this response after the round was complete]

Robinson: Did you have a bit of difficulty with the question?
Contestant: Yeah, but you asked me a difficult question. Everyone else got really easy questions and the question you asked me was, like, a million years old.

Robinson: No, no. Not quite a million years old. World War Two. Have you heard of that?
Contestant: It was after World War One . . .

Anne Robinson: Are you sure?
Contestant: Is that a trick question?

That's the trouble with history, isn't it? It's all about stuff that happened before you were born. And even when history isn't that ancient, did it really happen if it you didn't watch it on TV? That is the question prompted by this response from a local radio station in Bristol:

> **Host:** What happened in Dallas on 22 November 1963?
> **Contestant:** I don't know, I wasn't watching it then.

JFK's assassination in Dallas has been the source of a surprising amount of confusion on quiz shows, even when the presenter bends over backwards to help as in this moment on the radio station Magic:

> **Host:** In what year was President Kennedy assassinated?
> **Contestant:** Ummm . . .
>
> **Host:** Well, let's put it this way. He didn't see 1964.
> **Contestant:** [continues to pause for thought] 1965?

But surely everyone knows a bit about the two world wars of the twentieth century?

From *The Biggest Game in Town* (ITV)

Steve Le Fevre: What was signed to bring the First World War to an end in 1918?
Contestant: [looks up as though seeking inspiration] . . . Magna Carta?

From *Notts and Crosses* (BBC Radio)

Host: Where did the D-Day landings take place?
Contestant: Pearl Harbor.

From *Legends of the Hidden Temple* (Nickleodeon)

Olmec (the fictional host): Which of these men was a friend of Wild Bill and later fought a battle at Little Big Horn: General Grant, General Custer or Colonel Sanders?
Contestant: Colonel Sanders.

From *The Weakest Link* (BBC)

Anne Robinson: Name the Empress of Russia, who ruled between 1762 and 1796, and is famous for the number of her lovers.
Contestant: . . . Boadicea?

Robinson: According to the Bible, what city was destroyed along with Gomorrah?
Contestant: Atlantis.

Robinson: What is the round implement believed to have been invented around 4000 years ago and used in transport ever since?
Contestant: The steam engine?

Robinson: In Roman mythology, which animal brought up Romulus and Remus?
Contestant: A lion.

Robinson: In politics, what 'W' was a pact signed by the Soviet Union in 1955 as a response to West Germany joining NATO?
Contestant: The Williamsburg Treaty.

Robinson: What French word did Karl Marx use to describe those who oppressed the working class?
Contestant: Trotskyites?

Robinson: What religion was founded by the prophet Mohammed in 610 AD?
Contestant: Rastafarianism.

Robinson: Hadrian's Wall was built to keep out which tribe, the Picts or the Zulus?
Contestant: The Zulus.

Robinson: The name of which Italian, born in 1469, is synonymous with immoral cunning?
Contestant: Mussolini.

Robinson: In history, at the Battle of Waterloo, which general's horse was called Copenhagen?
Contestant: Lord Nelson.

In conclusion, quiz shows are clearly not the go-to place to brush up on your history. Often the problem is that quiz show contestants can't even distinguish between fiction and fact, as demonstrated in this answer:

From *In It to Win It* (BBC)

Dale Winton: In Shakespeare's play *A Midsummer Night's Dream*, who was the king of the fairies?
Contestant: I'm not very good at history.

* * *

HENRY VIII, AND COUNTING

You may already know one of the various mnemonics for King Henry VIII, which help store information about the monarch, for instance 'KTOT':

> King Henry VIII,
> To six wives he was wedded.
> One died, one survived,
> Two divorced, two beheaded.

Is there anything else you might need to remember?

From *The James O'Brien Show* (ITV)

James O'Brien: How many kings of England have been called Henry?
Contestant: Um, well I do know there was a Henry the Eighth . . .
O'Brien: . . .
Contestant: Errrrr . . . three?

From *The Neil Pringle Show* (BBC Radio)

Neil Pringle: How many strings does a guitar have?
Contestant: Er . . . four.
Pringle: It's the number of wives that Henry VIII had . . .
Contestant: Oh . . . five!

* * *

EVERYBODY NEEDS GOOD NEIGHBOURS

The following need no introduction and are all from the Australian version of *Family Feud* (originally on CBS).

Host: Name a celebrity known by only one name.
Contestant: Brangelina.

Host: Name something that increases and decreases in price as people buy and sell it.
Contestant: Weet-Bix!

Host: Name something you might freeze.
Contestant 1: Ice.
Contestant 2: Ice . . . Ice blocks?

Host: Name another word for 'Smart'.
Contestant 1: [after an agonizing pause, admits she can't think of anything]
Contestant 2: [who has misheard the question and thinks they have been asked for a rhyme] Dart!

Host: Name something you associate with a sauna.
Contestant: Bubbles.

Host: Name a type of badge.
Contestant: Chicken [in spite of repeated questioning, the contestant either refused, or was unable, to explain their thinking]

Host: Name something you associate with China.
Contestant 1: Thai food.

Host: Name something you might buy that could turn out to be fake.
Contestant: A car?

Host: Name something a woman carries in her
handbag . . .
Contestant: [buzzes in far too quickly] Mace?

Host: [finishing the question] Name something a
woman carries in her handbag that a man carries
in his pocket. Show me mace!

Host: Name something you might see in the
Wild West.
Contestant: A lion.

Host: Name an occupation that . . .
Contestant: [buzzes in then face-palms] A nurse?

Host: Show me a nurse! Name an occupation that
requires *a drill*.

Host: Name something you need to wash a car.
Contestant: A car!

Host: Name a fictitious creature that has wings.
Contestant: A unicorn.

Host: Name an animal that walks on two legs.
Contestant 1: A giraffe.
Contestant 2: A frog.
Contestant 3: An alligator.

Host: Name something that has spikes.
Contestant: A bicycle?

Host: Name something measured in metres.
Contestant: Parking.

Host: Name something that lives in a pen.
Contestant: Penguins?

Host: Apart from a foal, name a baby animal.
Contestant 1: A chicken?
Contestant 2: What's a baby lamb called . . .

Host: Name a famous landmark that's not man-made.
Contestant: Mount Rushmore.

Host: Besides meat, name something vegans don't eat.
Contestant: Chicken.

Host: Name a classic French dish.
Contestant: Ravioli.

Host: Name a sport in which animals compete.
Contestant: Duck shooting?

Host: Well. . . it's a very one-sided competition . . . I can imagine the ducks going, 'You just wait until we get our guns!'

Host: What's something you associate with Captain Cook?

Contestant 1: A hook.

Contestant 2: A . . . hook?

Host: Name one of the world's largest creatures.

Contestant 1: A bear.

Contestant 2: A crocodile.

Host: Name something you might find in ancient Greece.

Contestant: Ruins.*

* This was actually the top answer on the board, suggesting the audience (who had supplied that answer) imagined that the Ancient Greeks deliberately built and lived in ruins.

Host: Name a game you can play in the pool.

Contestant: Beach volleyball.

Host: Name something in an aquarium that a fish might not realize is fake.

Contestant: Alligator!

CALLING CAPTAIN OBVIOUS

There are times on game shows when it feels as though contestants, faced with the yawning emptiness of their minds, can think of no other option than to call on Captain Obvious to provide their answer. For instance, on the short-lived game show *Fort Boyard* (originally French and called *Les Cles Fort Boyard*; then English), host Melinda Messenger asked the contestant to rearrange the two groups of letters – CHED and PIT – together to form a word. Their answer was simply CHEDPIT.

Such simple repetitions of part of the question are one manifestation of the panic that leads to a visit from Captain Obvious. At the other extreme, we see contestants who are confronted with an incredibly obvious question, but then the mind rebels, fearing a trap, and they manage to somehow avoid the right answer. For instance, when one contestant on *The Weakest Link* (BBC) was asked which month of the year was named after the Roman Emperor Augustus Caesar, the clue really was in the name, but the contestant, after a moment's hesitation, plumped for . . . 'June'. It gets worse:

From *The Weakest Link* (BBC)

Anne Robinson: In the TV series of the same name, who played the pathologist Quincy?
Contestant: Quincy.

Robinson: What sign of the zodiac is represented by a fish?
Contestant: The Zodiac.

Robinson: In fashion, what is the French for 'ready to wear'?
Contestant: Pret à Manger.

Robinson: The name of which Caribbean island literally means 'rich port' in Spanish?
Contestant: Port Richmond.

Robinson: Name a selection of small, highly coloured sweets known as Dolly . . .
Contestant: Parton.

Robinson: In which year of the 1990s did badminton and basketball become Olympic medal sports?
Contestant: 1984?

Robinson: Complete the title of this Destiny's Child song, 'Bills, Bills . . . '.
Contestant: Don't know.

Robinson: What was the sequel to the movie *I Know What You Did Last Summer*?
Contestant: *I Know What You Did Last Winter.*

Robinson: Which Cluedo character has a military rank?
Answer: Colonel Sanders.

Robinson: In which movie did Harry Lime say, 'In Switzerland they had brotherly love and they had 500 years of democracy and peace. And what did they produce? The cuckoo clock!'?

Contestant: . . . *One Flew over the Cuckoo Clock?*

Maybe it's best to assume that the contestant in this instance was someone who worked in business and had read a lot of sales manuals in their time:

Robinson: Which 'B' completes the title of the book by Lord Baden-Powell: *Scouting For . . .?*
Contestant: Business.

Robinson: In his 1961 number one UK single 'Wooden Heart', Elvis sings in English and which other European language?
Contestant: English.

Robinson: What is the more common name given to the government department 'Military Intelligence Six'?
Contestant: MI5.

On another occasion, a contestant on the same show was asked what the 'M' in MI5 and MI6 stands for and answered, 'Murder'!

From *Family Feud* (CBS)

Host: Who do you think is responsible for the oil shortage?

Answer: Lack of oil.

The beauty of the next moment is seeing how the contestant simply jiggled around with the name of Notre-Dame to come up with a famous historical figure who unfortunately has absolutely nothing to do with the actual question:

From *Brainteaser* (Channel 5)

Presenter: Which literary hunchback lived in Notre-Dame and fell in love with Esmerelda?
Contestant: Nostradamus.

From *The Richard Allinson Show* (BBC Radio)

Allinson: What international brand shares its name with the Greek goddess of victory?
Contestant: [long pause] . . . Kelloggs?

From *Fifteen to One* (Channel 4):

William G. Stewart: Which cathedral town on the River Severn shares its name with the sauce used in a Bloody Mary?
Contestant: Tomato.

As the above answers suggest, a moment's thought would occasionally show the aspiring quiz show winner that they were on the wrong path. For instance, one contestant was asked what implement is used to warn athletes that they are about to start the final lap and answered, 'Starter Gun'. Similarly, the contestant who was asked 'Single combat is a fight between how many people?' might later have reflected that they should have thought for another moment before answering, 'One person'. And there is a certain bravado to this answer from *Steve Wright in the Afternoon* (BBC Radio), as the contestant is at least adding a small piece of information that isn't explicitly contained in the question:

Steve Wright: Who played agent 007 in the 1989 film *Licence to Kill*?
Contestant: Er . . . James Bond?

And finally, why wouldn't this contestant's guess be true?

From *The Dave Lee Travis Show*
(Breeze FM)

Travis: In which European country are there people called Walloons?
Contestant: Wales.

***

INADVERTENT BLASPHEMY

I'm not sure what the definition of blasphemy is now, but I suspect that this answer from *Steve Wright in the Afternoon* (BBC Radio) is at least edging close to the line:

Wright: Johnny Weissmuller died on this day. Which jungle-swinging character clad only in a loincloth did he play?
Contestant: Jesus?

***

DESPERATE MEASURES

One of the joys of quiz shows is the way they give us a chance to forensically examine the workings of the human mind. In particular it is interesting to note the creativity or weird lateral thinking that is deployed when a contestant feels cornered, hopeless or defeated. For instance, one contestant who, when asked to name the composer of *The Magic Flute*, hesitated before blurting out 'bikini' (Sigmund Freud would clearly have had fun with that). How to explain? Do contestants simply not want to admit how ignorant they are, and opt for what they hope will be a reasonable guess? Let's suppose that the contestant couldn't think of one single composer. Cue desperation, which insists that the brain at least invent something that sounds like a composer. And what do composer's names sound like . . . well, opera is Italian, and what sounds Italian? Words end ending in 'ini' – '*crostini*', '*panini*' hence . . . 'bikini'!

So, the moment of desperation can lead to answers that are wildly wrong but that at least have an element of inventiveness. But it can also lead to more of a 'rabbit in the headlights' approach, in which the contestant simply repeats part of the question as an answer, or latches on to the one part of the question that they have registered. For instance, there's the contestant who, when asked for the name of Kent's county town answered, 'Kentish Town'. Or the contestant who was asked for the South American country named after Simon Bolivar, and simply ran a memory search for the name of 'any South American country' and blurted out 'Brazil'. Here are a few more questions and answers that suggest the contestant has resorted to desperate measures:

From *The Weakest Link* (BBC)

Anne Robinson: In an orchestra, the leader normally plays which instrument?
Contestant: The triangle.

Robinson: The four Gospels of the New Testament are attributed to Matthew, Mark, John and who?
Contestant: [looking completely vacant] Joe?

Robinson: In which country is the River Po?
Contestant: ...

Anne Robinson: [says nothing, but raises a sceptical eyebrow]
Contestant: Poland?

Robinson: 'Bolster' is an anagram of which marine crustacean?
Contestant: Crab.

Robinson: What name is given to the field of medicine that concerns the health of women?
Contestant: Womenology?

Robinson: What 'Z' is used to describe a human who has returned from the dead?
Contestant: Unicorn.

Robinson: Who wrote *Cat on a Hot Tin Roof*?
Contestant: Dr Seuss.

Robinson: Who initiated the Chinese cultural revolution?
Contestant: Ming?

Robinson: According to the common saying, 'Revenge is a dish best served . . .', cold or on toast?
Contestant: [confidently] On toast.

Another contestant was asked 'Which organ of the human body is used for smelling and breathing?' Their answer – 'The lungs' – makes perfect sense if you assume that they weren't really listening and just latched on to 'breathing'. Or perhaps they were thinking about quirky ingredients for dinner! And in *Playing for Time* (BBC), the host asked, 'What letter is used twice in the word fillet?' The contestant looked pensive for a split second, leading the viewer to assume they were spelling out the word to themselves, before exclaiming 'Fish'.

The people who set quiz questions sometimes take advantage of the way that contestants panic to deliberately tempt them into looking foolish. For instance, it is common for panicking contestants to latch onto some element of the question and answer it with a kind of free association, starting from whatever bit of information lodged in their brain. So, if you want to throw a contestant off the scent when it comes to Roman poetry, it's a good idea to use the TV show *Thuunderbirds* to fog up and misdirect the brain.

Robinson: Which Roman poet wrote the Aeneid – Virgil or Brains?
Contestant: . . . [brain whirring] . . . Brains.

Robinson: In physics, which property of the moving body is measured in metres per second?
Contestant: Atom.

Robinson: If two opposite angles of a parallelogram are 70° each, how many degrees each are the two other angles?
Contestant: [eyes dart around as they replay words from the question in their head] . . . Seventy?

And this is one of my favourites, if only for the sheer ingenuity of the contestant's answer:

Host: Ken Follett is a famous what, author or photographer?
Contestant: Authographer?

And on the subject of getting desperate, or being driven mad, what about those contestants who keep saying the same thing, over and over again, expecting different results. This is amply demonstrated in those game show moments where contestants, behaving like rabbits caught in the headlights, find themselves unable to think of a different answer. Let's start with:

From *The Chase* (ITV)

Bradley Walsh: *The Vicar of Dibley* was set in what county?
Chaser Paul Sinha: [dramatic pause as this is a win or lose moment in the show] Berkshire?

Walsh: Incorrect. Same question to you, Rachel, Janice and Hugh.
Rachel, Janice and Hugh: . . . Berkshire?

From *Wheel of Fortune* (CBS)

On one occasion the contestants were confronted with the following board, and had to guess the well-known expression:

THE P_ _NTED DESERT

Lindsey (first contestant): The pointed desert.
Pat Sajak (host): That is incorrect . . .

James (next contestant): The pointed desert.
Sajak: That is incorrect, but you still have time to give me an alternate answer.

James: . . .the POINTED Desert?
Sajak: That's incorrect, no matter how many times you say it . . .

Final Contestant: The PAINTED desert.
Sajak: [rolls eyes in obvious relief]

In fact the host Pat Sajak has had his patience tried on many occasions. Witness this scene in which the contestant's witless attempts at being amusing would drive anyone to distraction. The board started out reading:

_ _ _ _ **N** _   _

_ _ _ _ _   _ _ _ _ _

Contestant A: Riding a brown horse?
Sajak: That's amazing, and it's wrong!*

Contestant B: 'G'
Sajak: One 'G'.

_ _ _ _ **N G** _

_ _ _ _ _   _ _ _ _ _

Contestant B: Riding a white horse?
Sajak: Who said anything about a horse? [after extended laughter, he walks off the stage]

* The correct answer was 'Seeing a buddy movie'.

This 1980s exchange from *Family Fortunes* (ITV) between the urbane light entertainer Max Bygraves and contestant Bob Johnson has been so widely reported that it effectively became a pre-internet, viral video meme:

Max Bygraves: Name something people take with them to the beach?
Johnson: Turkey [he scored 0 points].

Bygraves: The first thing you buy at a supermarket?
Johnson: Turkey [another 0 points].

Bygraves: A food often stuffed?
Johnson: Turkey [21 points].

Johnson's moment of madness does have an explanation. Apparently he hadn't had the isolation headphones correctly applied and overheard the third answer, 'chicken', from a previous contestant. In a panic, he assumed it was the first question, went with 'turkey' and kept on going as a kind of double or bust strategy.

In the little remembered ITV quiz show *Quizmania*, one contestant was asked for an occupation beginning with the letter 'T':

Contestant: Doctor.
Host: No, that's 'T' . . . 'T' for Tommy.

Contestant: . . .
Host: 'T' for Tango.

Contestant: . . .
Host: [getting desperate] 'T' for tintinnabulation.
Contestant: Oh, right . . . Doctor.

MAN, THE RATIONAL ANIMAL

There is sometimes an unspoken assumption that mankind is gradually getting smarter, and that the most intelligent humans today will be like children when compared to the intellectual elites of tomorrow. Unfortunately, the evidence suggests otherwise: it seems that we stopped getting smarter sometime along the path from the invention of the light bulb to the declaration of the First World War, to the widespread availability of TV and then, the final straw, the birth of the internet and social media.

The proof of this hypothesis is all around us, from the election of President Trump to the fact that the younger generation are incapable of finding their way half a mile across a city without staring at their phones all the way. But if you want a clinching bit of evidence, think about the future. If you survive the pandemic and lockdown and live on in a world where, say, scientists have been banned and you have to build a future society with an average group of people, as represented by contestants on game shows, what chance would they have of keeping the electricity working and growing enough food? Imagine trying to achieve that with the people whose answers to questions on science and the wider world are below. Scary, eh?

From *The Weakest Link* (BBC)

Anne Robinson: According to the proverb, the daily consumption of which piece of fruit keeps the doctor away?
Contestant: Banana.

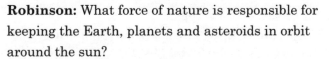

Robinson: What force of nature is responsible for keeping the Earth, planets and asteroids in orbit around the sun?
Contestant: Delta Force.*

* Of course, if Donald Trump had been the contestant he might well have answered 'Space Force', the name he has given his new branch of the military which has essentially been tasked with going where no man has gone before and fighting imaginary future wars in the cosmos.

Robinson: In science, what is botany the study of?
Caroline O'Shea (a media personality who had appeared on *Big Brother*): Bottoms?

Robinson: In chemistry, what do the letters 'Fe'
stand for?
Contestant: Silver.

Robinson: Which Italian city is overlooked by
Mount Vesuvius?
Contestant: Bombay.

Robinson: Which 'S' is the only country to have a
land border with Portugal?
Contestant: [stares into space, as though studying
an imaginary map] . . . Pass.

Robinson: What part of the human body is closest
to the floor when we are walking?
Contestant: The head.

From *Live and Kicking* (BBC)

Lara Crooks: What is the most abundant gas in
the atmosphere?
Contestant: . . . Air?

And what I love about this moment, again from
Live and Kicking, is the fact that the contestant has
given himself such a self-aggrandizing name. It'd be

interesting to see which direction Brainy would take if he was given the job of supporting a road trip to Mount Everest . . .

Host: Which mountain range separates France and Spain?
'Brainy Mechanic': The Himalayas.

From *The National Lottery Show* (BBC)

Host: What was invented in 1926 by John Logie Baird?
Contestant: Electricity.

From *RI:SE* (Channel 4)

Host: Where is the Sea of Tranquility?
Contestant: Ibiza.

Host: What prize did Albert Einstein win in 1921 for his work in physics?
Contestant: The Booker Prize.

Host: Name something that uses microchips.
Contestant: Deep-fat fryer.

From *Are You Smarter Than a 5th Grader?* (Fox)

Jeff Foxworthy: True of false, the oesophagus connects the mouth to the nose.*
Contestant (who happens to be a pre-med student): True.

Foxworthy: Thank God you are not my doctor! Did you go to any of your pre-med classes while you were there?

* The answer is false; it connects the mouth to the stomach.

Foxworthy: What planet in our solar system takes the least amount of time to orbit the Sun?
Contestant: I think it must be the Moon, because we see it every night.

From *The Nick Girdler Show*

(BBC Radio Solent)

Nick Girdler: I'm looking for an island in the Atlantic Ocean . . .
Contestant: . . .

Girdler: Its name includes the letter 'E'.
Contestant: Ghana?
Girdler: [with suppressed exasperation] No, listen . . . It's an island in the Atlantic Ocean [waits for the penny to drop].
Contestant: . . . New Zealand?

Host: Besides America, a country starting with the letter 'A'.
Contestant: Asia . . . Amsterdam!

From *The Chris Searle Show*

(BBC Radio Bristol)

Chris Searle: In which European country is Mount Etna?
Caller: Japan!

Searle: I did say 'which European country' . . . So, in case you didn't hear that, I can let you try again.
Caller: . . . ummm . . . Mexico?

* * *

CELESTIAL MOTIONS

One staggering moment in quiz show history came in an old episode of the UK game show *Bullseye* (ITV), when a contestant's belief that each country had its own sun, which revolved around it, became all too apparent. On the same topic, this question from *The Breakfast Show* (Wave FM) suggests that a bit of basic science education is still lacking in our schools:

Steve Powers: What does a planet orbit around?
Contestant 1: The galaxy.

Powers: No . . . I'll pass that over.
Contestant 2: The moon?

* * *

MATHS, *MILLIONAIRE* AND GOOD HUMOUR

There aren't many people who would enjoy having to perform mental arithmetic in front of an audience, so one can understand why brain freeze sets in when the subject of a round on *Who Wants to Be a Millionaire* (originally ITV before going multinational) is mathematical. The American actress Patricia Heaton experienced many people's worst nightmare on a celebrity edition of the show when she was raising money for charities working in Sierra Leone. She had made it to $25,000 and was facing the next question for $50,000. It's worth quoting at length, both to show the difficulties of trying to help out a contestant who is in the full throes of a panic and for how incredibly long it took her to reach the correct answer:

> **Patricia Heaton:** [on being asked how she felt by host Regis Philbin] Right . . . I don't know. I need a lot of help, because I went to Ohio State . . .
> so hopefully you're going to give me a really easy question, Regis, because if you don't then what's

going to happen is there's going to be some Sierra
Leoneans knocking at your door . . .

Regis: I don't know what the question is, I just
gotta ask you one question and if you can answer it
correctly we will give you $50,000 to split between
your two charities . . . you get to choose one of the
four lifelines – phone a friend, ask the audience,
and double dip or you can ask our experts. So . . .
let's play *Millionaire*!

Patricia: [immediately looks panicky seeing the
numbers in the question]

Regis: If a euro is worth $1.50 . . .

Patricia: Nooo . . . no. No.

Regis: Patricia, please stay with me . . . five euros
is worth (a) 30 quarters, (b) 50 dimes, (c) 70 nickels,
(d) 90 pennies?

Patricia: I'm nervous . . .

Regis: Why exactly?

Patricia: Ohio State! [audience laughter]

Regis: OK, so five euros will be worth how much at
$1.50 apiece.

Patricia: . . .

Regis. So, quarters now fifty times would be . . .

Patricia: I pay everything on credit cards! I have
no idea what . . .

Regis: So, 50 quarters would give you how much?

Patricia: Literally . . . my kids . . . once they got past second grade I could not help them at all with their math at all . . . I need to call my husband. He's European! [audience laughter]

Regis: [calls husband and asks him to stay on the line]

Patricia: There's people starving in Sierra Leone.

Regis: And we want to help them . . .

Dave (Patricia's husband): Hi Patty, hi Regis.

Regis: How are you doing tonight?

Dave: I'm . . . I'm actually nervous actually.

Regis: Now, we've got a question here that she just will not answer and she feels you can help . . . it's for $50,000 if you get the right answer.

Dave: OK, all right.

Regis: So, now you're gonna have thirty seconds and your time starts now . . .

Patricia: [gabbling so fast she is hard to understand] If the euro is worth $1.50, 5 euros is worth what, (a) 30 quarters, (b) 50 dimes, (c) 70 nickels or (d) 90 pennies?

Dave: [pauses] Sorry, just run through those again.

Patricia: [gabbles through the list even faster so that she is even harder to understand, but is cut off by the buzzer] Ohhh . . . [throwing in the towel] I'll throw in the other $25,000 . . .

Regis: [very, very calmly] The reality is that you have not given up and you haven't lost yet. You didn't say 'final answer'. . .

Patricia: Ohhh . . .

Regis: So, $25,000 but we can get $50,000. Just think about this so you don't lose . . .

Patricia: OK, so here we go so . . . 5 euros five times five is twenty-five carry the five . . . six . . . seven . . . $7.50 . . . I don't know.

Regis: 50 dimes is how much.

Patricia: [excruciating pause] 5 dollars! [audience applause]

Regis: And 90 pennies . . . how many pennies make a dollar?

Patricia: . . .

Regis: [raises his eyebrows] 100! All right! So, 70 nickels . . . how many nickels in a dollar?

Patricia: [mutters to herself] $3.50!

Regis: And . . . how many quarters in a dollar?
Patricia: [looking intensely relieved as the penny finally drops]: All right . . . my answer is . . . 30 quarters [extended audience applause, possibly slightly ironic].

Another contestant on the UK version of the show recently had a less laborious but equally embarrassing moment:

Jeremy Clarkson: In a standard game of Sudoku, what should the nine numbers in a single row add up to? Is it 40, 45, 50 or 55?
Contestant: Well, it's going to be $9 + 8 + 7 + 6 + 5 + 4 + 3 + 2 + 1$ but I just have to work that out and my maths is notoriously bad.

Clarkson: [gives intimidating look as she mutters to herself]
Contestant: Well, I have an answer in my head but . . . OK. 40, final answer.

Jeremy Clarkson: That's the wrong answer . . .

* * *

GRACE UNDER PRESSURE

And if all that maths, all that humiliation is driving you bonkers, how about a dash of sympathy (on a completely different subject) from the extraordinary Greta Thunberg.

When Andrea Henderson, star of the medical drama *Casualty*, recently appeared on the cerebral UK quiz show *Celebrity Mastermind* (both BBC), she was given the following question:

John Humphrys: The 2019 book entitled *No One is Too Small to Make a Difference* is a collection of speeches made by a Swedish climate change activist. What's her name?
Andrea Henderson: [shaking her head in confusion] Sharon?

The moment turned into a widely shared meme which, inevitably, given the way that modern social media works, led to some widespread, unpleasant trolling of the actress.

Happily, Thunberg saw the funny side and even changed her Twitter screen name to Sharon in sympathy. So the next time someone gets their maths wrong or gives a loony answer, be kind!

* * *

UNIVERSALLY CHALLENGED

Here are a few moments from *University Challenge* (BBC), which demonstrate the many pitfalls of agreeing to appear on a quiz show at all, let alone one that claims to be testing the intelligence and erudition of the participants. Many of these questions actually invite stupid answers, so the impressive thing is that in at least some cases the correct answer was given.

Bamber Gascoigne: If (a) stands for Artichoke, (b) Because, (c) Curriculum, and (d) Do, what might 'e' be for?*
Contestant: [the whole team looks round in panic and confusion and hesitates until one tentatively answers] . . . elephant?
Gascoigne: Correct . . .

* The stinger here is that any word starting with 'e' would have been correct since it was a random sequence.

Jeremy Paxman: Light travels 186,282 miles per second in a vacuum. How many miles does sound travel per second in the same conditions?
Captain of Manchester team: It doesn't travel at all in a vacuum.

* Which again is a correct answer to a trick question.

Here's one from the early days of the show, when editing out any bloopers or swear words was a complex process, thus the host's hasty bit of covering up:

Gascoigne: [asks a question to which the correct answer is the name of a German composer]
Contestant: [struggling to remember in frustration]: . . . Shit!

Gascoigne: No, it's not Schmidt.

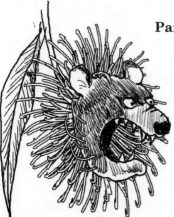

Paxman: Name the type of flower that grows in Tanzania and is named after both its area of origin and the colour of its petals.
Contestant: Tanzanian Devil?

And here's a case where a not unreasonable guess only succeeded in causing offence to the host:

Paxman: During which activity did some students stir up controversy for competing on behalf of Cambridge when they were in fact Oxford students?*
Team 1: The Boat Race?

Paxman: That's incorrect. . .
Team 2: [buzzing in] *University Challenge. . .?*

Jeremy Paxman: [clearly offended at the slur] Thank you very much!

* The correct answer was ballroom dancing.

Paxman: Who was on the British throne at the start of this millennium?
Team 1: Queen Victoria.

Paxman: [passes the question to the other team as this is incorrect]
Team 2: Ethelred The Unready.

Paxman: I know she was an old trout, but not that much of an old trout!

There are a few instances in which contestants on the show have given what appear to be stupid answers, but actually outsmart the host Jeremy Paxman (who has a supercilious persona, whatever he might be like in private). This first instance led to Lydia Wilson being voted Woman of the Week by BBC's *Woman's Hour* for standing up to Paxman:

Paxman: [the screen shows a British tourist sign, a symbol in the shape of an oak leaf] For ten points, simply tell me what it is.
Lydia Wilson (New Hall, Cambridge): It's an oak leaf [audience laughter].

Paxman: [disdainfully]: Anyone can see it's an oak leaf! I was asking what it was!
Wilson: You asked me what it was . . . You should have said, 'What is it for?' not 'What is it?'

Paxman: [in a huff, awards no points] It's a sign, signifying the National Trust. Actually, on a point of pedantry you may be right, but there you are, bad luck!

And in the second instance:

Paxman: Which planet is principally made of iron, but shares its name with a different metal?
Warren Read (Reading University): Pluto.*

Jeremy Paxman: [laughs disparagingly]

Read: Plutonium. It does share its name with a different metal – you can't argue with that!

Paxman: . . . Well, I suppose it does, if you want to treat it that liberally, but I'm not going to accept it – the answer's 'Mercury!'

* Incidentally, for any ultra-pedants out there, Pluto was still classified as a planet at this point, although it has now been reclassified as a dwarf planet.

And on a more radical note, Manchester University was banned from the quiz in 1976 when their team wanted to protest against what they perceived as the show's elitism; they answered either 'Marx' or 'Trotsky' to every single question. The university did not appear again on the show until 1996!

FAMILY FEUD REVISITED

Before we move on, here are just a few more pearls from the treasure trove that is *Family Feud* (CBS). Of course the whole point of this show is that you have to guess what the most common answer given by a group of people might be, meaning that you aren't being asked to be smart, in fact you are being asked to guess the lowest common denominator. But it still throws up some bizarre answers on a very regular basis. The answers here go back from Steve Harvey to the original host, Richard Dawson:

Steve Harvey: Fill in the blank . . . Raging what?
Female contestant: Raging ho!

Harvey: [contemplative pause] . . . Are you going through something? All the answers the other day, 'All men are dogs', now we're talking about this little 'Raging ho' . . . what the hell happened?
Contestant: It's the first thing that came to my mind!

Harvey: How is 'Raging ho' the first thing that comes to anybody's mind? I ain't even heard of it before! If it was up there, I'd have made them turn around . . . [chuckling] Raging ho!

Harvey: Name the most important woman in America.
Contestant 1: My mom.
Contestant 2: My wife.

Harvey: Name a birthday that many people are too depressed to celebrate.
Contestant 1: Valentine's Day.
Contestant 2: Birthdays.

Harvey: Name a real animal people tattoo on their bodies.
Contestant: Unicorn.

Harvey: Fill in the blank. If I could eat all I want of one food without getting fat, I would choose . . . what?
Contestant 2: Water.

Harvey: At what age is wearing a bikini for most women not an option.
Contestant: Seventeen?

Harvey: Name something you do routinely every Saturday.
Contestant: Brush teeth.

Harvey: Name something you might put on top of a salad.
Contestant: Whipped Cream.
Harvey: My favourite! Whipped cream on a salad!

Harvey: Give me a man's name that's three letters long.
Contestant: Will.

Harvey: Name a place that women don't enjoy going to alone.
Contestant: A funeral.

Harvey: Name something people hope . . .
Contestant: [buzzing in] That they go to heaven [audience laughter].

Harvey: 'That they go to heaven'. Wait till you hear the rest of this question. Look at me. Name something people hope *a house guest doesn't do in the bed!*

Harvey: We talked to 100 women . . . Name something you can't wait to get out of at the end of your day.
Kevin: Marriage [camera pans to Kevin's wife, Terri, who is looking daggers at him and then to Harvey who is heartlessly laughing at the mess Kevin has got himself into].

Harvey: You know . . . Terri . . . Kevin was only answering from a *woman's perspective* because 100 women were surveyed.

Richard Dawson: Name something you may accidentally leave on all night.
Contestant: Your shoes.

Dawson: I hope you don't take this the wrong way, Kenneth, but you are weird [turns to look at answer board]. Shoes!

Dawson: Name something that can kill a lively party.
Contestant: A gun.

Dawson: Name something you squeeze.
Contestant: Peanut butter.
Dawson: You're very weird, honey.

Dawson: Name the first article of clothing you take off when you get home from work.
Contestant: Um, underwear? [audience laugh and she blushes] What am I saying?!

Dawson: Next question – what time do you get home from work?

Dawson: Name something you wash once a week.
Contestant: [buzzes]

Dawson: Claudia?
Claudia: Yourself.

Dawson: Yourself? . . . I will not be coming around.

Dawson: Name a piece of clothing wives buy for their husbands.

Female contestant: Halter tops . . . Ohhhh . . .

Dawson: I know when my wife bought me my very first, uh, halter top, I think I can honestly look back now and say that's where our relationship started to drift apart.

Richard Karn: Name a word that starts with the letter Q.

Contestant 1: Cute.

Contestant 2: Quizno's.

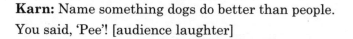

Karn: Name something dogs do better than people. You said, 'Pee'! [audience laughter]

Karn: They . . . they can do it better!

Contestant: They got a lotta different ways.

Karn: They, well . . . yeah! They got reasons, too!

Karn: Name a sport husbands and wives play together. You said . . . 'Kickball'! You know, you're not usually married in the 3rd Grade . . .

Karn: Name an animal you might see drinking out of a pond.
Contestant: Elephant.

Karn: Name the heaviest thing in your house.
Contestant: The dog.

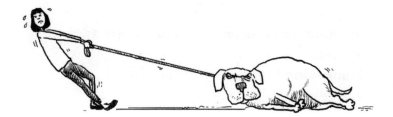

Richard Karn: Name a sport that is not played with a ball.
Contestant: Bowling.

Karn: Name an animal whose eggs you'd probably never eat for breakfast.
Contestant: Hamster.

Karn: A hamster?!
Contestant: [curls up in embarrassment]

Karn: I, I hate to tell you but, you know, those little pellets aren't eggs.

Karn: Name something you'd find in an operating room. You said: 'Operator'! Well, somebody's gotta operate! He's the operator!

Karn: Name a place where they sell cotton candy.
Contestant: Museum.

Ray Combs: A food that makes noise when you eat it.
Contestant: Um . . . a really loud hamburger!

Combs: Did he say it in time, judge? He said, 'a really loud hamburger'. [laughter]
Combs: [to contestant] That's called extra rare.

Combs: Give me another word for zero.
Contestant: Infinity.

Combs: Name a famous biblical duo.
Contestant: Laurel and Hardy.

Combs: I asked you to name a dangerous piece of playground equipment. You said, 'A tyre'.
Contestant: Well, if it's still attached to the car, it would be dangerous.

And now, to finish, an array of Q's and A's:

Q: Name a famous male dancer.
A: Betty Grable.

Q: Name something a woman might burn.
A: Her birth certificate.

Q: Name the most lovable breed of dog.
A: Kitten.

Q: Name a type of fly.
A: Butterfly.

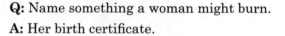

Q: Name a tradition associated with Christmas.
A: Hanukkah.

Q: Name something a guest might take home as a memento of a wedding.
A: The bride.

Q: Name something you might accidentally get hit by at the park.
A: A car.

Q: Name a sport where players wear gloves.
A: Badminton.

Q: Name something with a trunk.
A: Girl.

Q: Name something a pirate might lose in a fight.
A: The fight.

Q: Name an invention that has since replaced stairs.
A: The wheel.

Q: Tell me a bird that starts with the letter 'P'.
A: Flamingo.

Q: Name a state with the word 'New' in it.
A: New-braska.

Q: Name a fruit that starts with 'A'.
A: Arange?

Q: Name an occupation helicopters are used for.
A: Tuna fishing.

A FINAL THOUGHT

Throughout this book we have seen contestants who have given embarrassing answers to questions, many of which will haunt them in years to come as blooper reels on the internet enshrine and amplify their idiocy for everyone's entertainment. While this must be a mortifying experience, they can firstly console themselves that they have at least added to the general merriment for all. And when it comes to contestants like David Lammy and Monty Panesar, along with everyone else who has been seen to fail on quiz shows from *Mastermind* to *Who Wants to Be a Millionaire?,* they might take some comfort from the famous original presenter of *Mastermind,* Magnus Magnusson.

A talented journalist and presenter, he was best known and revered as the stern but avuncular host of the show in its early years. Incidentally, he once described how he had received an angry letter from a viewer accusing him of blasphemy for having read out that Jesus's first name was Reginald. He had actually been talking about the fictional P.G. Wodehouse character Jeeves! So it is worth remembering his most famous quote when asked about *Mastermind*: 'It's only a bloody game!'

ACKNOWLEDGEMENTS

Recently, as this book was about to go to press, I was gratified to watch one of the most impressive performances I've ever seen on *Who Wants to be a Millionaire?*. Donald Fear breezed through the questions from Jeremy Clarkson with remarkable insouciance and confidence. When it came to the crucial last two questions, Clarkson struggled to inject any note of tension into the proceedings. Fear, a history teacher, was asked about the politician who had held all four high offices of state: he clearly knew this was ex-Labour Prime Minister Jim Callaghan before the answers were even displayed. And when it came to the million-pound question, naming the pirate who had died in battle off the coast of North Carolina in 1718, he casually mentioned he had taught a course in piracy before reeling off the answer of Blackbeard in no time at all. A modest, quiet man, his main ambitions were to buy a motor home and 'give loads of it away'.

It made me reflect once more on the dynamics of game shows. The creators of these programmes put a lot of effort into making entertaining television, and we can all be grateful to them for the fun they have created. But at the same time, there is a certain gladiatorial aspect to these shows, in which we relish seeing the contestants sweating and struggling and, occasionally, making fools of themselves. A show like *Who Wants to be a Millionaire?,* more than any, deliberately cranks up the pressure: the contestant's chair is uncomfortable on purpose; the format, with the host and contestant face to face, is intimidating; and a simple question like 'is that your final answer?' would make anyone fall into a chasm of self-doubt. The joy of Mr Fear's performance was seeing someone who was entirely immune to the pressure, partly because he had the good fortune to have a series of questions to which he already knew the answers. But most contestants aren't so lucky, and part of the fun of watching the show is that slightly cruel amusement we get from watching them struggle, while at the same time learning a surprising amount about their individual personalities.

So, above all, I'd like to offer thanks and apologies to all of the contestants who have been described and quoted in this book. As viewers, we all know the answers when we are shouting at the TV screen, and if we don't, we can always reassure ourselves that we did. We weren't the ones who were under those bright lights, feeling our minds go blank at the key moment.

I'm sure my wife and daughter (whose patience while I wrote this book I was extremely grateful for:

ACKNOWLEDGEMENTS

I spent a large part of it sitting in the corner with headphones on, occasionally snickering to myself) would confirm: I can be a know-it-all. Maybe that's why I would never want to go on a game show to test myself out: I wouldn't want to be there in that moment, knowing that my inability to remember the answer to a simple question was being recorded for posterity.

Instead, I'll raise a glass to all the contestants, from the estimable Mr Fear to the most embarrassing of failures, for their bravery in taking the risk.